Words, Space, and the Audience

List of Previous Publications:

Reassessing the Theatre of the Absurd: Camus, Beckett, Ionesco, Genet, and Pinter

Refiguring Oscar Wilde's Salome (editor)

Eugene O'Neill's One-Act Plays: New Critical Perspectives (co-editor)

Words, Space, and the Audience

The Theatrical Tension between Empiricism and Rationalism

Michael Y. Bennett

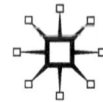

WORDS, SPACE, AND THE AUDIENCE
Copyright © 2012 by Michael Y. Bennett

All rights reserved.

First published in 2012 by
PALGRAVE MACMILLAN®
in the United States—a division of St. Martin's Press LLC,
175 Fifth Avenue, New York, NY 10010.

Where this book is distributed in the UK, Europe and the rest of the
World, this is by Palgrave Macmillan, a division of Macmillan Publishers
Limited, registered in England, company number 785998, of Houndmills,
Basingstoke, Hampshire RG21 6XS.

Palgrave Macmillan is the global academic imprint of the above
companies and has companies and representatives throughout the world.

Palgrave® and Macmillan® are registered trademarks in the United
States, the United Kingdom, Europe and other countries.

ISBN: 978–0–230–11680–1

Library of Congress Cataloging-in-Publication Data

Bennett, Michael Y., 1980–
   Words, space, and the audience : the theatrical tension between
empiricism and rationalism / Michael Y. Bennett.
     p. cm.
   Includes bibliographical references.
   ISBN 978–0–230–11680–1 (alk. paper)
   1. Theater—Philosophy. 2. Theater audiences—Psychology.
3. Drama—History and criticism. I. Title.
PN2039.B46 2012
822'.909—dc23   2011052922

A catalogue record of the book is available from the British Library.

Design by Integra Software Services

First edition: July 2012

To my sister, Anna, who taught me the wonder of expressing art through music, and my grandmother, Doris, who taught her family the wonderment of words.

Contents

Acknowledgments	ix
Introduction: Words, Space, and the Audience	1
1 Victorian Ideals: Wilde Performances in *The Importance of Being Earnest* and *Salome*	27
2 After the Great War: Contextualizing the *Self* in Italy and *Six Characters in Search of an Author*	57
3 1952 Paris: *Waiting for Godot* and the Great Quarrel	81
4 Cold War Tactics: Fear in *Who's Afraid of Virginia Woolf?*	103
Conclusion: The Epistemological Quandary over Improvisation, Impermanence, and Lack of a Script in Performance Art—An Interview with Coco Fusco	125
Notes	135
Bibliography	169
Index	177

Acknowledgments

This book is a product many years in the making. The idea for this book came from a deleted section from my dissertation chapter on Ionesco's *Rhinoceros*. Using this deleted section as my inspiration, I spent five years formulating, constantly reworking, and rewriting literally one paragraph that outlined the project of this book. The full conception of this book project came to me only a few days after the acceptance of my first book, *Reassessing the Theatre of the Absurd* (Palgrave Macmillan 2011). For this current book, I have been helped countless times by numerous individuals. This book could never have been completed without the help of all of the following people and opportunities.

I would like to thank Coco Fusco (Parsons School of Design) for her willingness to be interviewed; Bruce Bashford (Stony Brook University), who read multiple drafts of Chapter 1 on *Earnest* and provided me with essential comments for revision; Joseph Bristow (UCLA), who helped me find out more information about the influence the Oxford idealists and F. H. Bradley had on Wilde and Walter Pater, Wilde's most influential professor and mentor (a vital connection that I was unable to draw myself), and who reminded me about Wilde's reference to Hegel at the end of the revised version of Wilde's "The Truth of Masks," and told me about the existence of Wilde's "Notebook on philosophy" at UCLA's Clark Library; Joseph Donohue (UMASS, Amherst), who directed me to an invaluable source on Wilde's notes from college; Richard Allen Cave (Royal Holloway, University of London), who directed me to scholarship on what books Wilde read; Dustin Friedman—who is writing a dissertation entitled "Negative Eroticism: Sex, Aesthetics, and Critical Subjectivity, 1864–1896" at UCLA—for his deep knowledge of Wilde's connection to idealism and the numerous sources that he alerted me to; Timothy Chambers (formerly of the Philosophy Department at the University of Hartford) for helping me ensure that my philosophical arguments in Chapter 1 were sound and based upon scholarly philosophical conversations; Emma Kuby (History Department at UW-Whitewater), who provided me with a great reading list of books on the history of post-WWII France for Chapter 3; Stephen Bottoms (University of Leeds), who read a draft of Chapter 4 on *Who's Afraid of Virginia Woolf?* and provided me with essential comments for revision; Robert Combs (George Washington University) for helping me work through many ideas in this book; and Chris Calvert-Minor and David E. Cartwright (both in the Philosophy and Religious Studies Department at UW-Whitewater), who helped me understand the philosophical lines of influence since the revival of Hegel in the nineteenth century.

And extra special thanks go to Travis Tucker (Philosophy Department at the University of Hartford) for reading an *entire* draft of the book in order to ensure that my philosophical arguments were sound and based upon scholarly philosophical conversations; Donald Jellerson (English Department at UW-Whitewater) for reading a draft of the *entire* manuscript; Rebecca Hogan (English Department at UW-Whitewater) for reading drafts of the manuscript and making invaluable suggestions; Joseph Hogan (English Department at UW-Whitewater) for his tremendous editorial insights; David Reinhart (also in the Philosophy and Religious Studies Department at UW-Whitewater), who I team-taught a course with Spring 2011 called "World of Ideas: Memory, Truth, and Ethics," which provided me with a space to test out many of my ideas for this book in a university classroom setting; my research assistant, Kayla Corcoran, paid by a University of Wisconsin-Whitewater Undergraduate Research Assistantship grant; and the University of Wisconsin-Whitewater for a course release Spring 2011 and a Summer 2011 research stipend.

Finally, I wish to thank my friends and colleagues in the Department of Languages and Literatures at the University of Wisconsin-Whitewater, my friends, and my entire family for their constant love and support. I, especially, could not have completed this book without all of you.

Introduction: Words, Space, and the Audience

> In traditional Western theatre meaning typically emerges from the interaction of words and movement in the given space. Diction, intonation, and other paralinguistic features of the actors' delivery are obviously important factors in inflecting the meaning conveyed, but even more important is the spatial organization of the action for this can give specific meaning to the words spoken. With a different spatial organization the same words can be endowed with radically different meanings. Actors exploit possibilities arising from the position of speaker and listener(s) in the fictional world, movement or the lack of it, orientation, and the objects and elements around them in the presentational space in order to create meaning in relation to the words they speak.[1]
> —Gay McAuley, *Space in Performance*

> To be or not to be—that is the question...[2]
> —Hamlet, William Shakespeare, *Hamlet*

> ...an act hath three branches—to act, to do, to perform...[3]
> —Gravedigger, William Shakespeare, *Hamlet*

IN A LARGE SENSE, Gay McAuley summarizes my entire book in the above paragraph. McAuley's extensive look at space in performance (as his book is also aptly titled) makes the elements of the theatre speak to one another: how do words and space, for example, affect one another and the meaning of the performance? To a degree, my book simply goes deeper into the issues that McAuley raises. However, my book is also concerned with how we—the audience—*process* the juxtaposition of theatrical elements.

Especially since Bert O. States' *Great Awakenings in Little Rooms: On the Phenomenology of the Theatre* (1985), many theorists of the theatre (including McAuley) have turned to phenomenology to facilitate meaning. My book does not dismiss phenomenology—a type of empiricism—in favor of rationalism, for example, but suggests that the very nature of the theatre forces the audience to use *both* empirical and rational approaches to understand a play. I argue that some extremely influential modern plays not only force both the empirical and rational approaches, but actually take up their contemporary empirical versus rational debate: that the very plays are, to a large degree, philosophical inquiries into the age-old epistemological empirical versus rational debate.

Hamlet delivers one of the most famous lines in all of literature: "To be or not to be—that is the question . . . " The question of *being* and the idea of the essentialist characteristics of humanity come to the forefront of this soliloquy (and maybe the entire play). However, it is equally important to juxtapose the Gravedigger's philosophy about *action* (which he uses to suggest that Ophelia wittingly committed suicide and, thus, should not have a Christian burial). The idea that Ophelia's act somehow defines her and that she is a sinner in the eyes of others, casts the actions of *doing, acting,* and *performing* as determining existence: where, to use Sartre's idea, *existence precedes essence*. *Hamlet* is a play not just about being and doing, but how being and doing are understood (epistemologically) from the eyes of a beholder. Every one of the main characters is an observer, watching, trying to understand someone else: all of the main characters watch (or have another character watch) Hamlet, and Hamlet is watching Gertrude and Claudius. Thus, one through Hamlet and the other through the Gravedigger, Shakespeare presents the two sides of the age-old debate between the sense of *a priori* and of *a posteriori* knowledge, respectively.[4]

Some of the most influential plays of modern drama, I argue, continue this debate. These plays—*The Importance of Being Earnest, Six Characters in Search of an Author, Waiting for Godot*, and *Who's Afraid of Virginia Woolf?*—all take up this almost-universal epistemological question. However, their engagement with the debate is thoroughly couched in their own contemporary history and philosophical debates. Thus, these plays are decidedly products of their time, which adds a new layer of thought to McAuley's above analysis. By exploring the Actor-Audience Relationship, how the four elements of the theatre interconnect, and two major philosophical frames (i.e., empiricism and rationalism) through which to interpret a play, this book delves deeply into one of the most fundamental, illuminating, and complex questions of the theatre: how does meaning get made?

SMOKY JOE'S CAFE

I would like to start with a personal story, if I may, about seeing *Smokey Joe's Cafe* on Broadway sometime in the mid-1990s, when I was in my mid-teens. My *reaction* to this performance, though years later, served as the impetus for writing this book. I was born in New York City and grew up in West Hartford, CT. Living two hours from the city and having relatives on the Upper West Side, I was fortunate to grow up seeing plays and musicals on Broadway and "Shakespeare in the Park." On our way to see *Smoky Joe's Cafe*, not knowing what it was about, I asked my mom to tell me about the show. As I recalled at intermission, I thought that she told me it was a "typical musical." (My sister is four years younger than me and loved musicals, so we saw many of them.)

I remember us having great seats (not always typical since we usually bought our tickets at half price based upon availability at TKTS in Times Square): almost dead-center about ten rows back. I played the guitar (at the time, rock and blues) and, so, when the show started, I immediately loved it. Pretty soon into the show after one or two songs ended, one or two characters left the stage, one or two stayed on, and a couple of new characters came on. I was trying to follow the movement of the characters. I was having trouble establishing character because they kept coming and going on and off the stage. "The character development is horrible," I remember turning to my dad and saying after about 20 minutes. He agreed. About ten minutes later, I turned to him again and said, "this has a horrible plot." Again, he agreed. (These were about the most sophisticated observations I could make in my teens.)

At intermission, my mom asked what I thought of the show. I told her that I hated it: I loved the music, but there was no character development and no plot. She was a bit confused. "What kind of plot would there be in a musical revue?" she asked me. "Revue?

I thought you said it was a musical! I would have liked it if I had known that it was a revue!" I replied.

This event stuck with me throughout college, all of graduate school, and even now, as a modern drama faculty member at a university. How could I have hated the first half and loved the second just because the word "revue" was added to my consciousness? I watched two different shows that night: a horrible, undeveloped musical and a light, fun musical revue.

It is easy to pass this off as a simple misunderstanding. But I watched the same reality that my mom watched sitting just to my right. My experience was entirely different. My understanding of the show was entirely different. But, again, we saw and heard the exact same show. I have been trying to make sense of these two hours of my life ever since. This book is the product of this search.

THE THEATRICAL TENSION BETWEEN RATIONALISM AND EMPIRICISM

Within the "four walls" of the theatre, an age-old philosophical question plays out nightly in theatres around the world: what is brought by the audience to the theatre and what is learned at the theatre? This is a question as much for the scholar of theatre and drama as it is for the philosopher. The philosopher of epistemology puts this question in terms of *a priori* knowledge (rationalism) versus *a posteriori* knowledge (empiricism). The scholar of the theatre, on the other hand, sees the question as explorations of archetypes and human nature versus explorations of experientiality.

Because viewing a play seems to be such an *experience,* in order to complicate the notion of traditional theatre, it is imperative to ask a counterintuitive question: when does the "play" start and when does it end? Much like Lacan's "mirror stage," where there is misrecognition of the "I," it is naïve to think that a play is so rigidly an isolated, individual endeavor. In a sense, there is a similar misrecognition of the beginning, middle, and end of a play. It would appear, without further scrutiny, that the play begins when the curtains rise (should that be the mode in which the start of the play is to be announced) and ends when the curtains fall. However, I believe that thinking the play, especially one like Shakespeare's *Hamlet,* begins and ends within the span of a few hours is a *misrecognition of theatre*. In order to demonstrate the philosophical and theatrical conundrum in the question as to when a play begins and ends and the question of *a priori* versus *a posteriori* knowledge, I would like to take you through a typical visit to the theatre: say, for argument's sake, a production of *Hamlet* at a well-regarded regional theatre (i.e., a well-done professional production).

The scene: *Enter Barnardo and Francisco, two sentinels.* The words: "Who's there?" And with that *Hamlet* begins . . . correct? In a sense, yes. In another sense, no.

Let us rewind back, say, ten minutes. You have already made your way to your seats after driving to the theatre, picking up your tickets at will call, and stopping at the bathroom (in hopes that you can make it through the entire play to avoid waiting in the long line at intermission). You have ten minutes to kill. You open your Playbill, flip to read a few bios (how many of the actors have been in an episode of *Law and Order*? you wonder), see which restaurants are advertising, and close the Playbill again. There are still five minutes left. Your eyes start to wander: you look at the Proscenium Arch (wow, quite impressive, you think), then you look up at the ceiling to see the chandelier, and then you start people watching. What an outfit! I would not be caught dead wearing that! Oh, it is nice to see some teens in the audience with their parents. Oh, please no, I hope that really tall man walking in is not going to sit in the empty seat right in front of me! Oh no! He is coming closer. Phew, he is sitting across the aisle! Oh, the lights are dimming. The play is starting!

Let us now rewind back, say, two weeks. You open your city or state's newspaper and, if you are reading this book, you probably check the Arts section. Oh, so-and-so, the newspaper's drama critic, is reviewing the new production of *Hamlet*. Ah, she likes it! She thinks that the acting is fine, especially the actor playing Horatio, and that staging the play in the "Wild West" is a novel concept, but one that works for highlighting the lawlessness of power and royalty. We should definitely get tickets to this production, you think. You call this ticket office and are presented with a choice of seating options: all the way in the back, where you can see the whole stage well, but not the actors' faces too well; right in the middle of the orchestra section; or on the far left, but pretty close to the stage, where you can see the actors' expressions very well.

Let us now rewind back, say, X years, back to junior year of high school, to English class. You are reading *Hamlet* for the first time. Honestly, you understand little of it at the time, except for the Cliff Notes. Still, you now have at least encountered the words of the play you have heard so much about for years. You have a sense of the play, from trying to wade through Shakespeare's language, from what your teacher taught you, and from the fact that it is a Shakespearean tragedy and you know that at the end of Shakespeare's tragedies, everyone dies.

Shall we go further back, say, to the first time you remember one of your parents acting seemingly rash, to the first time you spurned the love of that second grader who you were not sure you were in love with or you despised, or to one of your wild temper tantrums? What if we go back to the natural connection when you were a baby to your mother and how you, as a baby, must have felt when she stopped breast-feeding you?

Starting with the scenario of you as a baby, the question is, do we already know the themes of *Hamlet* just because we are human or do we learn them from a very early age? Is the concept of motherly love (to a child) something innate, or does the baby learn this through the constant reinforcement of being breast-fed and held? Does the baby innately understand concepts of (perceived) betrayal (by the mother) when stopped being breast-fed, or is this how the child learns that concept? Are we wired to spurn love at a young age, or is this a socially and culturally learned phenomenon? Do we understand rashness because we ourselves are born with our own unique thresholds for acting rash, or do we only understand it because we perceive it in others?

In high school, most of us have a basic understanding of *Hamlet* before we even read the play. When we first encounter Shakespeare's arguably greatest tragedy, are the tragic twists and turns of the play something culturally learned or is tragedy something we innately understand? Do we have to learn that murder is wrong? Or do we have basic ethical principles wired into our brain to ensure the preservation of our species, and therefore, murder goes against our human nature? You had begun the process of understanding the unique facts of *Hamlet* in high school, but considering (most likely) that the play is still elusive to you (and it still eludes the greatest of all scholars on a regular basis, and hence, its deserved status as one of the world's greatest plays), what kind of conception do you have of the play? If you only understand some of the lines, then surely the *Hamlet* you understood in high school is not the same *Hamlet* you understand now.

When we read a review of a play such as *Hamlet,* or simply hear who is directing it, how might our newly formed preconceived notions of the production affect our first viewing of it? What if you hate the "Wild West" because, psychologically, the arbitrariness of lawlessness does not sit well with your need to follow rules? What if, on the other hand, you love the "Wild West" because you grew up watching Westerns on television? Our conception of the "Wild West" is surely learned, but our *understanding* of it may well be innate because although the social situation was different, humans still acted like humans.

Finally, before the show begins, we begin to take in the place and our fellow audience members because we subconsciously have to understand the little room in which we will witness this great reckoning. In a sense, we need our bearings before we suspend our disbelief.

The play now ends and the curtains fall. The play, as I hope you can see from the above, of course, is not exactly over. The actors come out and we are gently torn from this alternate reality back to our everyday lives. We talk about the production after the play, its merits and maybe what the director meant by this production. If meaningful in any way, the production stays with us the rest of our lives. However, our memory is selective and we highlight certain parts: parts that maybe affected us during the performance for their novelty, or parts that we so thoroughly understood at the time of the performance because they hit a particularly human tone. We know *Hamlet,* but how?

But in another way, the performance does not end when the curtains fall because theatre demands the eyes of an entire audience. One audience member has no ability to see theatre panoptically (nor does the soldier see the prison panoptically either, for it takes a network of soldiers to see all around the entire prison space that Foucault describes, as the single soldier still only takes in one angle of the circle).[5] Because of this, approaching the full totality of the theatre can only happen to the conglomerate of an *entire* audience (as each audience member only experiences a very specific side of the performance). Because of our own limits of experiencing a play, it is one reason why the audience member feels so compelled to continue discussing it. In a sense, the totality of the performance does exist during the performance, but *the totality of the performance is only epistemologically revealed after the performance* (i.e., through after-performance discussions, reading/writing reviews, reading/writing academic articles, not just from the audience, but from the participants in the theatrical even, too). The more that is written and discussed about the performance—from as many vantage points as possible—the more that the totality of the play is revealed and understood.[6]

Overview

The case of the schizophrenic is actually of vital interest to the theatre scholar. To the schizoid, he or she believes that something else happened/transpired (i.e., experiences a "reality" different from the same reality of a "healthy" human). To themselves, schizophrenics are defined by their action (what they believe took place.) To assert otherwise, is to assert the presence of some outer judge (i.e., God-like observer of absolutes). This, ultimately, becomes of interest for the theatre scholar because one cannot take in *all* of a play. Theatre becomes the gauge of phenomenology: the great tension of the theatre is that of Sartrean existential experience versus Camusian reasoning and meaning making. There are "objectively" identifiable elements in the theatre—dialogue, gesture, and space—but the combination of them creates a schizophrenic reality, in that essence—what is defined by one's or something's action (via existentialism)—becomes totally phenomenologically relative when in the presence of an audience. (Herbert Blau aptly notes in *The Audience* that "there is a fantasy of the public.") However, considering that the "reality" of the theatre is phenomenologically relative, how then do we make *meaning* out of the theatre without the use of reason and rational thought?

The central epistemological argument that this book puts forth is that in order to generate meaning in the theatre, there is an inherent, ever-present *tension* between empirical and rational ways of understanding a play; a tension between contingency and universality; a tension between context and the innate; and a tension between what is brought to, created at, and taken away from the theatre and what of the play still remains. It, then, becomes impossible to understand a play without understanding that the tension between empiricism and rationalism is inherent both in the theatre and in making meaning out of a play. Productions and their contemporary contexts come and go, but there exists some residual element of a play. Three productions of, let us say, *Godot* may look, sound, and mean something different, but they are all, nonetheless, productions of the play *Godot*. This book examines both the contingent historical and philosophical contexts to produce new readings, but it also deconstructs these contexts to see what innately remains, what is essential in the text.

In a sense, this book is a story about a centuries-old philosophical debate: rationalism versus empiricism. This debate, and the tension it has created for those in the theatre and those interpreting the theatre, traces its roots back to Greek drama (though Greek drama will be beyond the scope of this present investigation). Not exactly a history of the theatre, this book examines the twists and turns of the history of theatre and juxtaposes them with, most especially at its pinnacle, the contrast between Sartre and Camus, which, in some ways, brought rationalism and empiricism into their greatest relief (even though most educated people still conflate the two thinkers).

I will examine four of the most *influential* plays ever written—Shakespeare's *Hamlet*, Wilde's *The Importance of Being Earnest* (also using *Salome*), Pirandello's *Six Characters in Search of an Author*, Beckett's *Waiting for Godot*—and read them alongside their contemporary debates between rationalism and empiricism to show how these monumental achievements were a product of their time, but also universal in their epistemological quest to understand the world through a rational and/or empirical model. Though I will not go so far as to argue such, one possible implication here is that these plays may very well have been influential precisely because they (probably subconsciously) engaged in their contemporary epistemological debate.

There are a number of wonderful, seminal books that investigate some of the above-named individual aspects of the theatre (i.e., words, space, gesture, and the audience): Herbert Blau's *The Audience* (1990); Stanton B. Garner, Jr.'s, *Bodied Spaces: Phenomenology and Performance in Contemporary Drama* (1994); Una Chaudhuri's *Staging Place: The Geography of Modern Drama* (1997); Gay McAuley's *Space in Performance: Making Meaning in the Theatre* (2000); and maybe the greatest book ever written on the theatre, Bert O. States' *Great Awakenings in Little Rooms: On the Phenomenology of Theater* (1987). Unlike these other drama/theatre books (that examine, say, one element of the theatre through, say, phenomenology), this book does not attempt to read these plays through one or the other philosophy, but, instead, contends that these plays, themselves, through juxtaposing the four elements of the theatre, engage in their contemporary epistemological debates. This book examines, then, the most basic *tension* of the theatre: how is meaning in the theatre made?

This introduction is not intended to answer the above question: it merely attempts to bring up the issues that will be discussed in the following four chapters and the conclusion (i.e., the chapters are where the rational-empirical debate will play out in more detail). I am trying to elucidate the epistemological difficulties present in the theatre. Because theatre is made up of words, space, and gesture in front of an audience, I am looking at how these elements modify one another and how the gathering of knowledge is fraught with problems. The most basic example of this is when someone goes into a room before you do and says, "the room is dark." Considering that the overhead lights are off, but not noticing the fact that a few pole lamps are on, you will most likely agree with the other person because it was framed as "dark." The word "dark" modified the reality of the room, creating a relative, perceptual reality. The epistemological quandary becomes, then, did you reason it as dark (or viewed it as such because of your innate understanding of darkness) or did you experience it as dark? Some of theatre's most influential plays, I argue, contemplate the audience's relationship to the rational-empirical mode of processing words, space, and gesture.

In order to understand the rational-empirical debates that will play out in each chapter and the conclusion, it is necessary to contemplate some of the nuanced facets of understanding external stimuli. In the following section, I attempt to show how words, space, and gesture have a very *real* effect on each other and that juxtaposing these elements, colors "reality." I argue that this juxtaposition creates a *relative, perceptual reality*. Once I establish this idea, then I am able to move onto the audience's own relative relationship to the theatre. This section deals with how an audience member might process the juxtaposition of words, space, and gesture (i.e., what are the possible ways in which an audience member might process the external stimuli created by the juxtaposition of words, space, and gesture). Following the discussion of what happens in the mind/body of the audience, I turn to ideas of social/cultural constructions of meaning. The analysis of *theatricality* provides the audience member with a problematic filter (i.e., meaning is filtered, not only through the mind/body of the audience member, but it is also processed by society/culture in a particular way). The very idea of theatricality, that it is a shifting concept, raises an interesting question about whether theatre, itself, is a rational and/or empirical endeavor. The fundamental question this introduction (and the book) takes up is, does the audience member understand a play phenomenologically (i.e., the meaning is processed through new, *a posteriori*, sensory experiences), or does the audience member understand the play rationally (i.e., meaning is culled from reason and *a priori* knowledge)?

Words, Space, and Gesture (In Front of an "Audience")

Hamlet has a well-known, constant script, and because of that, the audience brings both knowledge and expectations to the theatre. To return to my viewing of *Smoky Joe's Cafe,* I had certain learned expectations of a "musical." I became quite familiar with the tropes of musicals. When I encountered, what I thought was a musical, the tropes that guided me were nowhere to be found. I viewed the revue with the framework of a musical, which caused much of my disappointment. However, the confusion created an exciting newness for me. For once, I went into the theatre confronted with a new, unexpected "form," if you will. (This must have been what it felt like for audiences to confront early productions of *Waiting for Godot*.) Thus, I had to balance the newness I was now experiencing with what I innately knew going into the production. When, at intermission, I was told that this was a revue, then I was able to recall the tropes of a musical revue. Even though I enjoyed *Smokey*

Joe's Cafe better after intermission, what was gained by the absence of tropes was lost once the tropes (and enjoyment) were recovered. The word "revue," placed in my consciousness alongside the reality playing out before me, created a relative, perceptual reality for me.

In order to investigate what was happening when "revue" was added to my consciousness (on top of the reality before me), I must explore how juxtaposing words, space, and gesture colors each other's "reality" in the mind of a perceiver. The audience (which implies a reader, as well) only has three main things at his or her disposal in order to understand the play: words, space, and gesture. In a sense, though, there are really only two, as gesture (unless written into the text and then, in that case, overlaps with words) is generally a choice made for a *specific* production by the actor/director, and while it illuminates the play, it is not necessarily part of the play, per se. And while space is semi-negotiable, stage directions do not (very) generally spell out the vast, vast majority of gestures (that are being made *every* moment of *every* production). Gesture, in this sense, will not be discussed as much in this book because it is so dependent on each actor for each specific performance. Thus, this book will examine the play (as a more permanent concept, rather than the more fleeting nature of performance) by showing how words and space in front of an audience "create" meaning. And, as I argue, the plays explored in this book actively debate whether meaning is created empirically or rationally. The initial questions that beg investigation are, what is the relationship between spoken language and symbolic language? How do words, gesture, and space affect one another? And do words, gesture, and space color the other's reality? Examining phenomenology and rationalism, if you will, in order to apply it to the work of Artaud and developing a better understanding of the theatre, I hope to show how the interconnectiveness of space, gesture, and words, especially in the presence of an audience, drastically affects meaning in the theatre.

Antonin Artaud's "First Manifesto" in the "Theatre of Cruelty" is a seminal work on the precepts of symbolic language in the theatre. However, in order to understand Artaud's contribution, it is also necessary to understand Richard Wagner by way of Adolphe Appia. Appia was a designer of Wagner's operas. Wagner's music-drama, according to Appia, was a purely expressive art form; music was sole expression. In his designing of Wagner's operas, Appia focused on banishing painting scenery from the stage and replacing it with plastic elements. In order for the actor to move *within* the set, three-dimensional sets were necessary. And even more important to Appia's design, light—both the presence and absence, and shades, of it—created a more emotional atmosphere. This creation of the modern stage space was necessary for Artaud to conceptualize the physicality of the theatre.

For Artaud, the theatre needed a language to get across its physical "expression in space."[7] Artaud's vision of the theatre served as a counterpoint to realism: "the theatre must pursue by all its means a reassertion not only of all the aspects of the objective and descriptive external world, but of the internal world, that is, of man considered metaphysically."[8] In order to explore the inner workings of the human psyche, Artaud theorized a spectacular theatre centered around bodies without the standard partition between audience and actors. The text of the play is only a springboard for action. Artaud, taking Appia's theory to its natural conclusion and writing somewhat against him, banished the idea of a set and created a theatre that existed somewhere "between dream and events."[9]

For Appia and Artaud, their theories created a more realistic, or, rather, a more metaphysically expressive theatre based on bodies and space. But Artaud's theatre is not without words. Dominique Q. Fisher, in *Staging of Language and Language(s) of the Stage,* argues that Artaud's theatre is a combination of poetry and theatre, where "the plastic elements of language (voice, noise, gesture) [exist] in space at the limit of the poetic and the theatrical in which language is atomized."[10] What is important about this fusion is that the theatrical sign is not linguistic, but visual, gestural, and auditory.[11] For Artaud, what he disliked was the mimetic quality of language. The body and gesture created a nonrepresentational language. However, "Bodily language in Artaud's work does not pertain to a real body but to a spatialized body of writing which the hieroglyphic character... acts out on stage."[12] The hieroglyphic character resembles something like Balinese dancers or Craig's "Supper-puppets," where these "bodies" break with the Western cultural model of representation.[13]

Artaud introduced giant mannequins when he staged Strindberg's *Songe,* in Vitrac's *Mystères de l'amour,* and also in *Les Cenci*. In addition to the mannequins, the decor was bare and objects were placed out of context. This was done to highlight the fictitious nature of the performance.[14] Also, "verbal intonations strongly punctuated by screams, gestures, and contortions" combined with these visual elements to spatialize language.[15] In his goal to critique the Western "sign," Artaud transformed the theatre through "transforming scenic language."[16] By displacing the abstract with the concrete through visual modes of representation, Artaud circulated signs through various systems of representation.[17] His nonverbal signs mediated the space between the concrete scenic place of the stage and the offstage, dramatic imaginary space "the spectator re-constructs from the signs of the performance."[18] Nonverbal language joined with verbal language to create a nonmimetic, but more truthful theatre.

Artaud is, obviously, writing, at least, an indirect response to Ferdinand de Saussure. Saussure argued that *"the sign is arbitrary."*[19] There is no connection between the word *mannequin* and the pronunciation of it. By eliminating verbal language and replacing the word *mannequin* with the actual thing, Artaud got rid of the arbitrariness of language and its faulty mimetic quality.

Theatre, for the vast majority of plays, as I argue, falls somewhere between stark realism and Artuad's Theatre of Cruelty. Even in realism, many of Artaud's principles of scenic language exist. In short, set and language are in a constant tug of meaning making. There almost always exist the faults of language with the reality of a prop, however, symbolic it may be. The basic question for theatre as a whole is, for example, what is the relationship between the word *rhinoceros* and the actions in space of the actors in Damashek's production of Eugene Ionesco's play by the same name? "These symptoms range from a budding forehead protrusion to stomping, shoving, snorting, trumpeting, and aggravated shuffling."[20] Taken separately, these actions are *real* unto themselves. They paint a thousand different pictures. Together, existing without words, they create some type of caricature: either totally mimetic of something (anti-Artaud) or nonsensical in their assembly, creating a nonverbal language (Artaud). With the word *rhinoceros,* these actions come together to *represent* and *modify* a rhinoceros. This word exists in this play to represent and modify the characters' actions in space and the process of meaning making. Acting is always an action in space coupled with language that comes together to form a reality about the other.

The reality of words and space do not, necessarily, change when placed together. The actions of the actor in portraying a rhinoceros exist as a reality of their own. The word *rhinoceros*, or rather, the enunciation of the word rhinoceros, exists as a reality of its own. As individual entities, the word and space exist separately in an absolute reality. However, together, *words and space create a perceptive, relational reality*.

In his book, *Great Awakenings in Little Rooms*, Bert O. States discusses, at base, the interconnectedness between the real world and the illusion of the theatre. Coming through the body of the actor, the illusion and reality are always present and absent in the body of the actor:

> The illusion has introduced something into itself to demonstrate its tolerance of *things*. It is not the world that has invaded the illusion; the illusion has stolen something from the world in order to display its own power.[21]

Illusion *uses* reality to heighten the illusion. States provides an example. Albee's park bench, or a room, for example, must justify their presence: "they must inhabit the people who inhabit them."[22] In this way, the scenery is part of the characters. Speaking of Shakespeare's (lack of) scenery, States suggests that it is the power of naming that shows that Shakespeare is exploiting the "imperfections" of the stage.[23] States suggests that Shakespeare's theatre is defined, in part, through the "tension between seeing and hearing."[24] In examining realism in Ibsen and Chekhov, States said that "The object of the realistic setting was not only to look like a real room but to collaborate in a new relationship between perceived space and heard language."[25] States gets us close to understanding the phenomenal world of the relationship between words and space. States' book is a brilliant phenomenological exploration into the theatre. However, my one criticism of the book is less a function of States' intention than a perceived imperfection with the methodology, that is, phenomenology. States divides the book into two sections: each section examines one main element of the theatre (i.e., "The Scene" and "The Actor"). Then each section phenomenologically investigates the subject in relation to another aspect of theatre. The problem that lies here within is, to turn to Heidegger, that the observer in this case is not Being, but Nothing. In simpler terms, the audience is the ultimate Other: Nothing. The audience, in general terms, is Nothing in that it constitutes a limitless potential. If the audience were fixed—if it indeed represented the fantasy of a public—if it represented Being and not Nothing, then a phenomenological reading could be done. Phenomenology is the subjective experience of Being. However, phenomenology cannot take into account the subjective experience of Nothing.

Newton and Locke argue that space is independent of matter. However, for Leibniz, the sensed relatedness of space and matter is a phenomenal event that goes through an observer:

> ... for Leibniz not merely the spatial-temporal form of experience, its spatial-temporal order or relatedness, arises completely within the active ego or monad, but also the empirical data functioning as the end-terms in this relatedness have a similar origin. And precisely because the relatedness is not a substance within which any other substance, material or mental, is located, but is instead entirely within the content of consciousness of the windowless monad, no alternative remains but to regard space as purely relational, having as the terms of its relatedness the phenomena of consciousness.

This in turn has the consequence of making matter as known by any scientific knower or observer purely phenomenal.[26]

Space and matter become intimately intertwined in the mind of an observer. Taken, by extension, to the theatre, words, space, and matter come together in the same *perceptual* and *relational* manner. The word *rhinoceros* and the mannerisms of the characters in the Damashek production only create a reality for the perceiver in their *relative* relationship to one another.

WHAT REMAINS? WHAT IS ESSENTIAL IN THEATRE?

While the amalgamation of words, space, and the audience (and gesture, too) creates a perceptual and relational reality in which to make meaning out of a play, there exists something essential in theatre: the dramatic text. The text is the text is the text, and its unchanging reality does not only support some rational path to understanding a play, but it provides theatre with something both residual and universal. Thus, while historical, societal, and intellectual contexts are lost to time (or at least can never fully be recovered), and thus the perceptual and relational realities contingent on those contexts are also somewhat lost, the text is the residue that binds these contexts together: the text remains.

In a large sense, then, one of the possible conclusions of my argument is that one *also* has to take into account the tension between the dramatic text and the theatrical performance in order to make meaning of a play. This is in some ways an obvious statement. However, we must consider that while actual contexts and performances are lost to the past (and can never *fully* be recaptured), the history and continuity of social contexts and performances affect later contexts and performances. In other words, a performance and its context are not strictly ephemeral. The history of performance, especially since the blossoming of theatrical reviews (not to mention technological advances to capture plays), has its own residue; past (especially notable) performances clearly live on in and affect current and future performances.

THE AUDIENCE'S RELATIVE RELATIONSHIP

It is important to establish the effect words, space, and gesture have on each other (in the presence of an audience), but it is of equal importance to understand the audience member and how he or she processes these stimuli. But even before this, we must establish the relationship between an actor and the audience (or audience member). And in order to do that, we must first start with a more general relationship: the Performer-Audience Relationship.

The idea of the Performer-Audience Relationship can be built effectively around Richard Bauman's concept of *performance:* in performance there is a consciousness of doubleness (the performer is both performing something and aware of the fact that he or she is performing something *for* an audience). This is a seminal idea that enlightens the idea about performance, but it does not fully explicate the relationship that emerges between that performer and the audience. The performer's very existence is *for* the audience; the audience *uses* the performer (for its own entertainment and/or (self) knowledge). No performer, no audience; no audience, no performer. The performer and the audience can feed off of each other: the greater the performance, the more the audience takes away from it; the more applause (which is generally the way an audience exists for the performer), the more the performer tries to give exactly what the audience wants. We can imagine a rock star singing much louder; a sprinter getting an extra boost from the roar of the crowd to sprint faster; and the emergence of "showboating" from boxers or a basketball player throwing down a slam-dunk-contest type of dunk during a game, which is entirely *for* the audience (where the audience also includes teammates and opponents), as the dunk counts for the same two points as a lay-up. (This Performer-Audience Relationship will be explored again in the conclusion on performance art.)

Much like the Performer-Audience Relationship, the Actor-Audience Relationship begins with the same equation. The actor's very existence is *for* the audience; the audience *uses* the actor (for its own entertainment and/or (self) knowledge). No actor, no audience; no audience, no actor. However, the Actor-Audience Relationship is mediated by words, space, and gesture; this is how meaning is interpreted by the audience. As Bert O. States so beautifully put it, the actor *is* the story he or she is telling.[27] This creates a unique power dynamic in an Actor-Audience Relationship: the audience has little-to-no effect on the doings/actions of the actor (as the actor in typical modern drama *generally* has a script to follow, and audience responses do little to change the performance, or an even better way to put it, do little to change the story). The quality of the performance of the actor may improve with audience support, but the story that is told through the actor is fundamentally the same. Yet, the actor is beholden to the audience for his or her existence. Though this equation illuminates the need for each other for each one's existence, this is also not an egalitarian relationship. The actor is the focus, "in the spotlight," but does not directly benefit. The audience is "hidden," but directly benefits. This is a symbiotic relationship in that the audience parasitically derives pleasure/knowledge from the actor, while the actor relies on the audience for the actor's continued existence. (We will see that this Actor-Audience Relationship is vital to understanding, especially, *The Importance of Being Earnest* and *Six Characters in Search of an Author*.)

There exists a fundamental divide in the two ways an audience member can make sense of the words, space, gestures of the actor: process *a posteriori* sensory experience or use reason and *a priori* knowledge. The case of space-perception offers the theorist of the theatre a unique way to understand the nature of the theatre. Viewing three-dimensional space presents a problem for the philosopher, both the empiricist and the rationalist. The prevailing philosophical problem derives from instances people are immediately presented with three-dimensional visual information. Two classic approaches (i.e., empiricist and rationalist approaches) that philosophers take are (1) perceptual experience is "sensation plus conception (or thought)," or (2) "perception essentially involves conceptualization."[28] How, though, do we make sense of sensations that are outside of our awareness in regard to perception (i.e., what happens in instances where conceptualization is impossible and we are presented with only sensations due to our unawareness of the visual information?)? A. D. Smith proposes that in order to view three dimensions, the world presents an external reference (intentionality) in that the objects that are viewed are distinct from the subject viewing them. Therefore, sensational properties are "representational" since these "objects sensorily appear to him."[29] Smith concludes that "visual experience is indeed representational, but that the objects represented, and indeed the entire space in which they are located are unreal."[30] In other words, the objects that we see are neither representational nor nonrepresentational, but the *experience* of visually perceiving objects is done representationally, even though the external objects themselves are, in essence, unreal.

This idea is significant for the theatre viewer in many respects. (1) In contrast to the television or movie screen that frames what you see, the lack of a frame in the theatre makes it impossible to perceive (with awareness) the totality of the play in front of you. However, that is not to say that we are not sensing visual information that we are not processing conceptually. (2) Related to the first point, the problem of the theatre is not what you see, but what you do not see, and the fact that *you do not have to see it*. In this sense, the theatre audience experiences entirely different realities and, therefore, perceives objects representationally in entirely different ways (much like the schizophrenic). (3) The two elements of the theatre that pertain to vision—space and gesture—in-and-of-themselves are neither representational nor nonrepresentational. In other words, an open mouth "means" nothing without other visual and sensory information. We only experience the representation of an open mouth when in the presence of more visual information. An open mouth *does not* contain the concept of rage, joy, fear, tiredness, boredom, et cetera. An open mouth is hardly a "concept." "Rage" and its concept, for example, only become experienced representationally when in the presence of, say, furrowed brows, redness in the face, and erratic movements. In this sense, to return to an earlier point, rage will only become a reality when the perceiver experiences the visual information relatively and relationally. And this goes back to the previous point: what if you were simply looking at the set and not at the characters the moment that one of the actors presented the character with a furrowed brow? Of course, that "act" transpired in reality, but since that particular audience member did not experience that visual cue, the reality of that production will be experienced entirely differently from the person sitting next to that particular audience member. In essence, every audience member experiences reality differently because what one sees and hears is different. Theatre (and performance art, and possibly dance, I suppose) is unique in its impossibility to consider its totality, especially because of its fleeting nature. Words can be captured on a page. Everyone can read every word. However, how is one to capture an ephemeral "event"? Videotaping the performance, in a sense, frames the play in a static way, and gives directorial control to the videographer, no matter how "objectively" he or she tries to shoot the performance. A play, one time only, exists uniquely for each spectator precisely in that particular space, position, and moment in time. (And this has nothing even to do with the "experiences" one brings with them.)

MAKING MEANING OUT OF THEATRE

Given the almost infinite specificity of each audience member (i.e., the almost infinite different experiences each audience member brings to the theatre on top of his or her innate human knowledge and how that affects the understanding of a solitary, fleeting performance), how does meaning get made, is in a sense, the question being asked by this seemingly esoteric philosophical conundrum. In the theatre, we must look to the contemporary debates between the empiricists and the rationalists. But we must also look, using the context of these debates, to the conflation of mimesis, performance, and theatricality, and then how these three elements in combination are understood by the playwright, the director, the actor(s), and the audience. In other words, meaning, though independent of intention, can be affected by the proposed intention of the playwright, director, and actor(s). Much like the debate that, most notably, Oscar Wilde set off, the ultimate meaning of a play has something (though not entirely) to do with the artists' understanding of whether the play is *art for art's sake,* or is *art for life's sake.* The sense of which one of the two the play is depends upon the text of the play, but even more importantly, in this case, upon the director and actor(s). As much as we would like to say that the text is central to the meaning of performed play, there are so many cases where plays were directed and performed with exact opposite messages. When performed, the meaning of the play has much more to do with the director's (and actors') sense of mimesis, performance, and theatricality. This idea of theatricality brings up issues of social and cultural knowledge.

Thomas Postlewait and Tracy C. Davis begin their coedited book, *Theatricality,* by discussing the impossibility of mimesis in the theatre in their introduction: "The theatre may imitate life (or some ideal), but like a metaphor the representation is always removed from its model, falling short of it."[31] Though not dealing explicitly with phenomenology, the authors echo the sentiments most developed by Bert O. States: there is an interplay between the real, the presentation, and the representation in the theatre. Postlewait and Davis address this fact in that they recall the "absence" of the referent.[32] They give a perfectly cogent example of this: "Thus, a man impersonating a woman may persuasively signify femaleness, and though he will never become a female, in theatricalizing one he deceives as to the very nature of the absence."[33] Postlewait and Davis note that, in the twentieth century, there were many movements that tried to deal with the problems of mimesis in the theatre. Jerzy Grotowski, Peter Brook, Richard Schechner, and Ariane Mnonchkine, for example, looked to ritual as a way to "revitalize theatrical performance."[34] August Strindberg, Edward

Gordon Craig, Nikolai Evreinov, Luigi Pirendello, Antonin Artaud, Bertolt Brecht, and Jerzy Grotowski, for example, highlighted the fact that we are all playing roles. These playwrights and theatre practitioners all developed something of an antitheatricality. These *alternatives* to mimesis beg the all important question:

> Does dramatic performance refer beyond itself to the world or does it serve to make explicit the theatrical aspects of presentation? On one side of this debate is the naturalistic idea of theatre (in writing style, acting, scenic codes); on the other side is the series of antirealist alternatives (such as symbolism, surrealism, and expressionism).[35]

These questions were the subject of debate in the theatre world really since the 1940s.

In 1940, Mordecai Gorelik commented on theatricalism in his feelings that "theatre is theatre, not life."[36] By midcentury, scholars and theatre practitioners saw a main division in the theatre world. There existed an "alternative between 'representational' and 'presentational' styles."[37] This came out of the historical progression dating back to Ibsen that Postlewait and Davis describe. The combination of realism (Ibsen and Chekhov) and historical antiquarianism (Shakespeare) produced a pictorialist set design. This was replaced by Granville Barker's symbolist revolution. Modernist stage design informed Appia and Craig's conception of the theatre. And finally, Brecht came along and created a theatre where "actors could signal the falsity or duality of their own acting, selectively helping spectators to reject empathy and identification."[38] However, as the authors note, "The concepts of *metadrama* (a play which comments upon the conventions of its genre) and *metatheatre* (a performance calling attention to the presentational aspects of theatre and its conventions in the moment of its transpiring) are hundreds of years old."[39] Many of the Senecan devices used in the Renaissance made the audience more aware of the falsity of the theatre, thus, serving as a simultaneous counter-challenge to theatre's detractors who argued for theatre's "dissembling inauthenticity" (15). As Lionel Abel defined the term *metadrama*, with *Hamlet*, Shakespeare created a new "intellectual" theatricality that created a new "dramatic self-consciousness."[40]

Postlewait and Davis return to defining the word *theatrical* by examining its shifting meaning between artifice and nature.[41] This highlighted the philosophical battle over appearance versus reality. In the early eighteenth century, theatrical was on the negative side of the debate. In the nineteenth century, there was a strong disapproval of the theatre in bourgeois society. Theatrical was associated with all negative connotations. But by the early twentieth century, theatrical started to denote a "mastery of skill."[42] Even though audiences were aware of the fact that the actor was dissembling, in a sense, the better the actor *acted,* the more theatrical the performance. This brings up a crucial point about theatricalism: "Each age has its own idea of what is natural and lifelike."[43] Theatricalism is a shifting concept depending on the current age.

Postlewait and Davis conclude their introduction with theatrical's alignment with the idea of performativity: "Instead of a theatre of the playwright, performance art tends to be a theatre of the performer/creator."[44] Performance art, then, creates a self-referential system that articulates the "performer's presence, the performer's body."[45] This makes the "gaze" a fundamental part of performance and thus the resulting binary awarenesses ("everyday space/representational space; reality/fiction; symbolic/indicative") are at the heart of theatricality.[46] Postlewait and Davis finally expand their idea of theatricality to the societal scope: "theatricality has been enlarged and applied to politics whereby political behavior and its defining rhetoric are seen as theatrical (especially in the modern age of media and advertising). In addition, the ideas of national identity and imagined history are constructed as modes of performed identities. The public realm is the performative realm."[47] Here theatrical and performative are almost one. Thus, as the authors conclude, both theatricality and performance have a shifting history that has been distinct yet conflated with "mimesis, role playing, theatrum mundi, the carnivalesque, metatheatre, spectacle, ritual behavior, and social ceremonies."[48] Theatricality's shifting history has profound implications for understanding the empiricism versus rationalism debate as it pertains to the theatre.

Empiricism versus Rationalism in the Theatre

To assert that theatricality is a shifting concept is to suggest that the nature of acting and receiving that knowledge is not an innate proposition. That is, the very fact that each age has a different sense of *theatrical* presupposes that each era gathers the knowledge *a posteriori*, as an empiricist would suggest. But the fact that acting appears to be a universal action, to the West, suggests that our "concept" of acting as an alternative mode of being is innate, *a priori*, suggesting an Innate Concept approach to rationalism via Plato.[49]

A similar argument can be made about the writing of plays. The fact that each era has shifting genres to express the feelings and thoughts of the playwright would suggest that these forms are learned through experience. Likewise, the universal nature of playwrighting as a mode of literary operation appears to be more or less innate. Of course, I realize that these broad generalizations are dangerous because of all of the possible objections to specific departures from movements. But departures are usually *reactions to* well-known concepts and trends. Thus, the exception, in a sense, proves the rule.

Given that the very nature of the theatre is fraught in a cosmic clash between empiricism and rationalism, it becomes all the more complicated when examining specific plays, specific actions, words, and so on, in relation to specific audience members. Though I am not a philosopher, just from hearing years of analysis of productions and plays from students, friends, and family, it certainly appears that person X may understand *Play Z* empirically while person Y may understand it rationally. And furthermore, person A may grasp Act I, scene 2 of *Play Z* empirically while Act I, scene 3 rationally.

This interdisciplinary book (which links the disparate fields of drama/theatre, history, and philosophy) offers the reader a new lens through which to examine some of the most influential and most widely studied modern plays. The frame and methodology that I have constructed—that is, using the four elements of the theatre to examine theatre's tension between empiricism and rationalism—get to the very heart of the theatre. This allows me to (1) discuss one of the most fundamental questions of the theatre—how does meaning get made in the theatre?—and (2) produce radically different, new readings of canonical plays.

* * *

The structure of each chapter in this book is consistent. I begin each chapter with a brief political, economic, and cultural history to contextualize each particular time period. Then I move to the intellectual history that opens up each respective, contemporary debate between empiricism and rationalism. Finally, taking the history and philosophy as the context, I perform an in-depth close reading of each play. It should be noted here that my primary audience is drama and theatre scholars. Therefore, my historical analyses are not meant to add to the historical scholarly conversation, but are, instead, meant to help contextualize the period for the philosophers and the drama/theatre scholars. The same concept is true with the philosophy sections: the philosophy is not for philosophers, but historians and drama/theatre scholars. The close readings, however, *are* intended to add to drama/theatre scholarship. In each chapter, the sum total of the parts is meant to enlighten all three fields, as the discussion of each field provides a new sense of context for the other fields.

The four main chapters that constitute this book center around four tremendously influential plays: Oscar Wilde's *The Importance of Being Earnest* (1895) in Chapter 1, Luigi Pirandello's *Six Characters in Search of an Author* (1921) in Chapter 2, Samuel Beckett's *Waiting for Godot* (1952) in Chapter 3, and Edward Albee's *Who's Afraid of Virginia Woolf?* (1962) in Chapter 4. These plays were not just chosen for their thematic similarities (i.e., they appear to converse about rationalism and empiricism). Each of these plays first appeared in a place and time that represented a crossroads in history and philosophy. *These chapters trace the waxing and waning of rationalism and empiricism in key historical moments:* from the height of British Idealism and the birth of both pragmatism and analytic philosophy in 1895 England (which was at the very height of the "Gay 90s" in the *fin de siècle*); to the height of pragmatism, the concrete formation of analytic philosophy, and the death of idealism in 1921 Italy (which saw the birth of fascism and Mussolini's power after WWI); to the height of Sartrean existentialism and Camus' reaction to it in 1952 Paris (which was just beginning the economic rebuilding of France after WWII); and both the death *and* normalization of analytic philosophy in 1962 United States (which was in the very midst of the Cold War and still prospering after WWII). These chapters weave in and out of philosophical lines of influence (and some of the reactions to these philosophical lines): British Idealism's chain of T. H. Green to F. H. Bradley; analytic philosophy's line of Gottlob Frege to Bertrand Russell to Ludwig

Wittgenstein; the line of phenomenology from Edmund Husserl to Martin Heidegger to Maurice Merleau-Ponty and Jean-Paul Sartre (and Albert Camus' oppositional reaction to this line); and the various pragmatist movements (American, British, and Italian). The book ends with an interview with the performance artist Coco Fusco.

CHAPTER 1

VICTORIAN IDEALS: WILDE PERFORMANCES IN *THE IMPORTANCE OF BEING EARNEST* AND *SALOME*

HAMLET SAYS IT BEST: "To be or not to be—that is the question."[1] Oscar Wilde dramatizes this line in both *The Importance of Being Earnest* and *Salome*. However, I believe that Wilde takes Shakespeare's line even one step further. Wilde contemplates the idea of *both* possibilities: to be *and* not to be (simultaneously). By juxtaposing these two disparate plays and bringing them into a productive dialogue with one another through the contemplation of "performances" and the "gaze," we can see that Wilde meditates on the awful predicament found in his (and still our) society: Wilde suggests that as long as we live in a society where we cannot be true to our desires, in a sense, we are all damned to live in "bad faith," both *being* and *not being* ourselves.

In this chapter, I use the language of *Earnest* to read both plays. In this sense, "being earnest" is being true to oneself, not performing for someone else's sake or for society's sake. In fact, a close reading of the two plays shows that a society based upon false performances creates a world where desires are never met. Ultimately, both Algernon and Jack (in *The Importance of Being Earnest*) and Salome (in *Salome*) are forced to don another costume and speak in a language not their own in order to have their desires met.[2]

In *Earnest* and *Salome*, Wilde, I argue, anticipates a concept that was not fully articulated for quite some time: Sartre's idea of "bad faith." Wilde explores the not-yet-articulated idea of "bad faith" through portraying, what I call, *insincere performances* (cases where a person knowingly *performs* in "bad faith"). Exploring the concept of *insincere performance* helps us understand how Wilde engaged in both the political and philosophical debates of his time, and helps us draw these two *Wilde-ly* divergent plays into a productive dialogue that helps us reassess Wilde's oeuvre.

Though much of this chapter discusses *being*, and thus this chapter falls into the realm of ontology, the focus on the "gaze" (that is especially relevant in *Salome* scholarship and which I suggest should also be of great importance in *Earnest*) raises important epistemological issues. To a large degree, in front of a "gaze," *performances of the self* shape both how the subject is viewed by others and how the subject views him or herself. However, from an epistemological viewpoint, the question becomes, how is *being* understood? An examination of Victorian and *fin de siècle* England and the influence of T. H. Green and F. H. Bradley (whose idealism is written in response to British empiricists like Locke and Hume) on the British academy, particularly at Oxford—where Wilde spent four years—informs my reading of *The Importance of Being Earnest* and *Salome*.

The Left and the Right in Victorian and *fin de siècle* England

The *Belle Époque*, as late Victorian and *fin de siècle* England came to be known, was surprisingly *not* a period of tremendous economic growth. In fact, following decades of industrial prosperity, a great depression began in 1873 and lasted until 1896. Even though there was general agreement about the existence of a depression, by most criteria, the era was still prosperous, as demonstrated by the growth of Friendly Societies and savings banks, increases in tea consumption and sugar, more travel, and no decreases in the number of servants, licenses to shoot, and the number of carriages.[3] Much of the depression was due to the fact that "Britain was suffering from having had her industrial revolution first": Britain's well-established industries, which were prosperous, were also inelastic in their ability to adapt to new methods of production.[4] One place Britain looked for economic relief was to its vast Imperial Empire.[5]

Though the plight of Britain's colonized people was not subject to reforms, near the end of the century when the people of Britain were exposed to a depression, there was an interest in reforming the relationship between capitalism and labor: "In the kind of language [the unskilled workers] were beginning to use, they were prosperous when capitalism was expanding and the margin of concession was high, but they were the first to be sacrificed when capitalism contracted and the margin of concession was low."[6] The depression allowed people "to question the basis upon which their society was built," and led not just workers, but also intellectuals, to ponder the chances of the survival of a capitalist society.[7]

The result of the Socialist revival was the formation of two political and social identities: one on the Left, and one of a somewhat-reactionary Tory identity on the Right. Matthew Fforde paints two wonderful pictures of these oppositional political and social identities. The Right, in Fforde's view, was concerned with a type of *laissez-faire* society with the focus on the individual, who was kept in check through a sense of personal duty and virtue:

> On the Right there was a desire to leave the individual free from government and to stress that national advance could be achieved by correct individual activity within the community at large. "Negative" liberty and personal duty were the cornerstone concepts of this decided individualism. The cultivation of individual virtue was a necessary goal because only in this way could duties be properly discharged—hence, in part, the ideal of the "gentleman." Such voluntaryism looked to the proper exercise of freedom of will in all spheres. "Nation" was a much more attractive concept than "society." The emphasis was upon belonging (and the actual state of belonging was of crucial importance) to an integrated and integrating nation composed of individuals aware of their private and public duties; motivated by a strong sense of citizenship; and bound together by special customs, traditions, and mutual obligations... Underpinning this individualism, voluntaryism and communitarianism were the accompanying beliefs that man had free will, a spiritual dimension, and a social nature.[8]

This Right, Fforde says, desired to achieve a "nation" based upon a sense of individual duty. Because of its focus on the individual and free will, a sense of individual virtue was necessary. The nation, then, would be virtuous because of its virtuous, gentlemanly citizens.

On the other hand, for Fforde, the Left was more interested in building a society than a nation, with the exact opposite implications for the role of the individual:

> On the Left there was a tendency to see man as an outcome of societal forces, to conceive of society in terms of conflicting socio-economic groupings, to emphasize the role of material wealth in human fulfillment and motivation, and to stress the need for the individual to aid others by supporting statist action. Such materialism, determinism and classism gave rise to a desire to liberate the individual from economic conditions and to restructure the material bases of society. Citizens would achieve "positive" liberty through government action. Much was implied in these tenets. The ground was prepared for relativism. Individuals were seen in relation to their class of their society. Egalitarianism was supported by a tendency to evaluate economic status as the outcome of external conditions and not internal ability. DeChristianisation was encouraged—man was to look to the state, not God for immediate improvement.[9]

Unlike their counterparts on the Right, the Left focused on the state and society for aiding individuals, who were seen as a product of societal forces. These societal forces, mostly because of unfair economic conditions, were to blame for wide gaps in the quality of life for the rich and poor: the state, then, should restructure the material base of society to ensure an egalitarian society.

This clear split in ideology between the Left and the Right not only influenced the political and economic climate of *fin de siècle* England, but it was a reflection of the current debates going on in philosophical circles. While I may make a passing remark here and there about the Left versus Right in relation to *Earnest*, I am not introducing the concept of Left versus Right in order to set up a reading specifically of *Earnest*. Rather, I am suggesting that the social and political debates between the Left and Right in Victorian England were echoed in the emergence of British Idealism. Though the philosophical debate (i.e., the emergence of British Idealism in the face of British empiricism) was not a Left or a Right debate, it was, however, a debate that focused on the role of the *individual,* especially in regard to knowledge and morality.

1895 England was an *almost*-prelapsarian moment. The "Gay 90s" and the *belle époque* were in their final struggle-for-existence. *Earnest* embodied all of the hope and excitement of the age, but equally hinted at what was soon to come within the next few years. In 1895, the British Liberal prime minister, William Gladstone, and his party lost to conservative Unionist, the third Marquess of Salisbury. And by 1902 and 1903, respectively, the almost unilateral strength of British Idealism was shaken by the introduction of American pragmatism by F. C. S. Schiller and then Bertrand Russell's *The Principles of Mathematics.*

BRITISH IDEALISM

The renewed focus on the individual (and some of the ethical implications derived from it) from both the Left and the Right went hand in hand with the Neo-Hegelian principles that were being raised by the British Idealists at the same time. The key to understanding British Idealism is that it was a response to/refutation of British empiricism and also British materialism—which espoused that all knowledge comes only to the senses from the material world—which, as a form of empiricism, was much more the dominant strain of empiricism in the late nineteenth century. Though it is always hard to pin exact dates for the genesis of almost anything, one likely candidate for a formal beginning to British Idealism is T. H. Green's massive (371-page), 1874 introduction to David Hume's *Treatise of Human Nature.* (David Hume [1711–1776], many times grouped alongside John Locke (1632–1704) and other British empiricists, was one of the key empiricists of the eighteenth century.) Green's intended purpose, at the time, was not as much to develop a philosophy of his own, but to calm the brewing religious crisis of the age. Green—a former student of Benjamin Jowett and a Fellow at Oxford, who preceded William Wallace as Whyte professor of moral philosophy—thought that Hume was unable to resolve both science and religion (because of Hume's perceived unclear sense of knowledge and morality). According to Frederick Copleston, Green suggested that since empiricism cannot explain the existence of knowledge and morality, one should look to the philosophies of Kant and Hegel, instead.[10]

Green's idealism became more concrete with his book *Prolegomena to Ethics* published posthumously in 1883. Green takes up the subject-object relationship from an epistemological view, similar to other early idealists. For Green, for something to be real, according to Frederick Copleston, it has to come from the order of Nature (i.e., a member of a system of relations). However, just because one is aware of a series of related events does not mean that that awareness constitutes that series. The mind actively synthesizes nature, but the mind itself is irreducible to that which it synthesizes: consciousness is irreducible to anything else. Green suggests that while each finite mind/consciousness conceives Nature as a system of relations, there must exist an eternal consciousness that produces/constitutes Nature. This eternal consciousness, or God, reproduces its own knowledge in finite minds (through our ability to perceive and respond to stimuli). Human consciousness is made up of both empirical and metaphysical aspects: empirically, consciousness comes forth through the "successive modifications of the animal organism"; metaphysically, humans become "the vehicle of an eternally complete consciousness."[11]

The same year as the appearance of Green's introduction to Hume's book, F. H. Bradley made his first significant contribution to philosophy. Though his 1874 essay "The Presuppositions of Critical History" did not introduce the idea of the "Absolute" that Bradley came to be known for, it did lay the groundwork for Bradley's future philosophic thought, which reached its height in influence in the 1890s (at the time of Wilde's composition of *Earnest* and *Salome*). Bradley's idea of the Absolute, his hallmark contribution to British Idealism, comes most particularly from his 1893 book, *Appearance and Reality*. For Bradley, according to Copleston, reality is one; it is the splintering of reality into finite parts (which are connected by relations) that constitutes appearance. Simply, then, the Absolute is the totality of its appearances.[12]

It is difficult to know how much Bradley's philosophy (especially *Appearance and Reality*) influenced Wilde's two plays at all. However, Wilde's long engagement with philosophical conversations and the intellectual world that Wilde continued to inhabit after his time at Trinity College, Dublin, and Oxford would suggest that he *may* have been at least familiar with this very influential text. I introduce Bradley not to suggest that Bradley's philosophy definitely influenced Wilde, but that his philosophy was in the air around the time of *Earnest* and *Salome*. As will be shown in the next section, Wilde was clearly well read in and a part of the philosophical world of the Oxford Hegelians (as well as their idealist responses to materialism, which Wilde also had some familiarity with). It is important to note the connections between all of the philosophers and Wilde: both Wilde and Green were students of Benjamin Jowett (at different times), and Wilde was a student of William Wallace, who took over Green's seat as the Whyte professor of moral philosophy at Oxford. This overlap of philosophic minds did not end just with the above philosophers. Wilde had a veritable onslaught of mentors who made significant contributions to late nineteenth-century British Idealism (and a few who contributed, on the other hand, to materialism, including his closest mentor, Walter Pater).

Oscar Wilde's *The Importance of Being Earnest* and *Salome*

At Trinity College, Dublin (1870–1874), Wilde was mentored by J. P. Mahaffy, a Kantian idealist, and was a member of the University Philosophical Society at Trinity; thus, he began his immersion in the philosophical debates of his time. While Wilde was at Oxford University (1874–1878), Oxford was the intellectual hotbed of British Idealism, and Wilde was certainly influenced by this philosophical movement.[13] Wilde met John Ruskin while studying with Wilde's first idealist mentor at Oxford, the eminent comparative philologist F. Max Müller.[14] Like Müller, Ruskin was an idealist, but Ruskin was also someone who opposed the materialism of modern science. It was the intellectual debates between Ruskin and Walter Pater at Oxford that gave Wilde a perspective on the two sides of the idealist-materialist debate. The debate between Ruskin and Pater centered around two opposing views of Aristotle's *Ethics*, the most translated Greek philosophical text in the nineteenth century and required reading in Oxford's *Literae Humaniores* program.[15] Wilde, who had read and carefully studied *Ethics*, would have been well aware of the divergent positions taken by Ruskin and Pater.[16] While Ruskin attacked what he perceived was the materialist base of the Aesthetic movement, in Pater's "Conclusion" to *The Renaissance* (1873), Pater "makes a materialist, relativist, and subjectivist argument":

> This interpretation allows Pater to claim that the cultivation of consciousness—the maximizing of an individual's experience by being "present always at the focus where the greatest number of vital forces unite in their purest energy"—is "success in life." Because of his materialist perspective, Pater rejects "philosophical theories or ideas," any "facile orthodoxy, of Comte, or of Hegel, or of our own"....[17]

Though Pater was Wilde's closest mentor at Oxford, Wilde's own notes in his notebook entitled "Commonplace Book" implicitly suggest that Wilde adopts the importance of the *theoria* interpretation of Ruskin over the importance that Pater gave to *energia*, with both *theoria* and *energia* discussed in *Ethics;* thus, because of this alignment, Wilde clearly placed himself in the camp of the Oxford Hegelians.[18]

Wilde's two most significant influences from the Oxford Hegelians came from the previously mentioned William Wallace and Benjamin Jowett.[19] The Oxford Hegelians, by and large, solved the classic philosophical problem of the relation of Being and Not-Being by suggesting that "truth was a dialectical relation of Being and Not-Being."[20] This pervading Hegelian theory also helped bridge the problem of evolution: "natural selection also posited a world of flux which evolved through a process of conflict."[21] Wilde synthesized Wallace and Jowett's Hegelian theory, which provided Wilde with a type of idealism—which allowed the incorporation of materialist assumption and findings of science (especially with regard to evolutionary theory)—that he found preferable to that of Müller and Ruskin.[22]

Though Wilde's time ended at Oxford in 1878, which preceded the most important works of, arguably, the most influential British Idealist, F. H. Bradley, Wilde's interest in philosophy, especially in Hegel, continued. In 1891, in his revised essay, "The Truth of Masks," Wilde concludes the essay with maybe the essay's most Wildean (Hegelian) turn, where one can firmly see the profound impact that Hegel had on Wilde's view of art and truth:

> Not that I agree with everything that I have said in this essay. There is much with which I entirely disagree. The essay simply represents an artistic standpoint, and in aesthetic criticism attitude is everything. For in art there is no such thing as a universal truth. A Truth in art is that whose contradictory is also true. And just as it is only in art-criticism, and through it, that we can apprehend the Platonic theory of ideas, so it is only in art-criticism, and through it, that we can realize Hegel's system of contraries. The truths of metaphysics are the truths of masks.[23]

Though Wilde clearly sided with the Oxford Hegelians, Wilde's knowledge of T. H. Huxley—whose 1879 book on the British empiricist David Hume (which Wilde read) established Huxley's idealism as a materialism—and Wilde's own synthesis of idealism with a touch of materialism, led Wilde to respect the truth and authority of modern science, but that "idealists should rush in where materialists feared to tread when the constraints of materialists' assumptions prevented them from explaining certain human psychological experiences."[24]

In the opening scene in *The Importance of Being Earnest* (which I will return to again), Algernon is playing the piano, presumably poorly. To his butler, Lane, Algernon says, "As far as the piano is concerned, sentiment is my forte. I keep science for Life."[25] In the previous quote from Algernon and in the above quote from Wilde's "The Truth of Masks," we encounter some of Wilde's own philosophical contradictions that take the form of an Hegelian dialectic.[26] However, here, Wilde's dialectical method undermines even an Hegelian idealist philosophy. There is a *hint* of an idealist-materialist divide in what Algernon says: here, art is antimaterialist (in the realm of "sentiment," in the mind) and "Life" is implied as having a touch of the materialism associated with the (rules of) "science" that Wilde *did* accept. But as Wilde says about art, "A Truth in art is that whose contradictory is also true," we are able to imagine—especially given the fact that "in aesthetic criticism attitude is everything" and, in a sense, Algernon is performing a bit of aesthetic criticism on himself—that the idealist-materialist divide can also be read in such a way where the reverse is also true: by capitalizing the "l" in "Life," Wilde turns the word into something of an abstract concept, and thus, this passage suggests that since "science" is used "for" Life, at base, the realm of Life falls into idealism, while the materialism associated with "science" is merely *used* by Life, as science is something *for* life. This oppositional dialectic that Wilde constructs in this quote contains a bit of both Huxley's concept that that idealism can exist for a materialist and Wilde's own (above) conclusion that a materialistic science can still be valid for a Hegelian idealist.

Though, personally, Wilde was clearly of the Hegelian idealist ilk (though, Wilde, like almost all other philosophers was rarely totally uniformly this or that), Wilde does not write *Earnest* or *Salome* as tracts on Hegelian idealism. Instead, and in the true spirit of Hegel, Wilde presents the tension between idealism and empiricism (in this case, materialism). In order to advance Hegelian ideas, Wilde realized that he also needed to juxtapose these ideas with the tenets of materialism. Hence, the main plot (though, in a sense, least important from a deeper perspective) focuses on the philosophical tension between idea and fact: the tension between the *idea* (as a rational concept) that Jack is Ernest and the *fact* (as an observable, tangible truth) that Jack is actually named Ernest. Although both the idea/concept and the fact that Jack is Ernest are true at the end of the play, it turns out that the fact that Jack was always Ernest was all that mattered to produce a happy ending: for it was Lady Bracknell who needed Jack's name to be Ernest to be fact. However, the very notion that it is Lady Bracknell who is associated with fact suggests that Wilde, ultimately, sides with Hegelian ideals, as who in the audience would ever side with Lady Bracknell (as she is presented as a satire of her class and herself). Wilde hated *facts*: "For Wilde, as for Kant, facts were highly problematic entities; moreover, if they remained unilluminated by philosophic theories, they were meaningless. 'Facts,' as he put it, 'are the Labyrinth: ideas the guiding thread.'"[27] Thus, the audience, not via Wilde suggesting as much, would have come to its own conclusion (via the dialectical narrative arc) that the *idea/concept of being Ernest/earnest* is much more important than the *fact of being Ernest*.

In *The Importance of Being Earnest,* Wilde, I contend, was contemplating the tensions between British Hegelian Idealism and British materialism (empiricism). However, if we bring the debate between the British Left and Right to bear on this play, we may hazard to suggest that Wilde did take issue with Victorian England's obsession with the ideal and the subsequent societal "gaze" that resulted from it. While not taking sides between the Left and the Right in his two plays, Wilde does interrogate the contemporary problems through the same lens of individuality. Wilde, of course, fully engaged with this idea in his 1891 essay "The Soul of Man under socialism." Wilde, however, at least according to the portraits of the Left and the Right drawn by Fforde, was not a typical Socialist in that Wilde strove for the individualism of the Right, while suggesting that the means to achieving individuality was through the Left's political and economic project. As Fforde describes it, on the Right, there is an emphasis on the individual. However, the individual must conform to/strive toward an ideal. As will be discussed, in the *insincere performances* by Algernon, Jack, and Salome striving for an ideal, they must be aware that they are simultaneously *being themselves* and *being who they are not*. On the other hand, the stilted language that does not change with Algernon, Jack, and Salome's change of location suggests the problems with the Left's notion of relativism. When each character's situation changes, the worldview of the Left would suggest that they should change with their surroundings. But the fact that there is a constant among these characters also defies the notion of relativism and the de-emphasis on the individual, however problematic Wilde portrays individuality. Wilde, then, indirectly addresses both the Left and the Right, but does not side with either, finding problems with both, in terms of their engagement with individuality. Philosophically, Wilde, much more directly, engages his contemporary epistemological debate in much the same manner.

To be perfectly honest, my arguments here have very little to no precedent in performance. This play, which is performed in numerous community theatres (and described by Alvin Klein of *The New York Times* as "an all-too-often produced comedy"[28]), has been typecast, I guess you could say, as a witty comedy (with a hint of satire).[29] And that is not to suggest that it is not that (i.e., a witty comedy). However, my concern is that *because* it is such a perfect witty comedy, it becomes too easy to miss the play's complexity and deeply philosophical observations. Maybe that is why there has been only one performance review of the play in the academic journal *Theatre Journal;* directors are simply missing that the play has something other to say than its wit. Sara Freeman, in her review in *Theatre Journal,* laments, one could say, that seeing such a play as *Earnest* "makes contemporary comedy seem not only dreary, but without philosophy."[30] Though Freeman's review does discuss the innovative use of physicality in this production directed by Charles Newell,[31] much to my disappointment, the review does not discuss exactly how *Earnest* is *with philosophy* (in contrast to contemporary comedy).

However, I was fortunate enough to see the 2011 production of *The Importance of Being Earnest* by Roundabout Theatre Company in New York City.[32] In many respects, this production was remarkably un-noteworthy. Despite the casting and marvelous acting of Brian Bedford as Lady Bracknell, the director and actors played the play "straight." What was noteworthy in this production, however, were the very subtle acting choices made by Santino Fontana (Algernon) and David Furr (Jack). Fontana's Algernon was wide-eyed and fully manic, while Furr's Jack was as grim, serious, and somber as one could imagine. These two acting choices had profound implications for the interpretation of this staging of the play. Algernon's gestural mania suggests that he was not in full control of reason: his wit becomes a sign for the audience, not of profundity, but of grandiose irrationality (though one can see the trace of the rational in what Algernon says, in mania, the irrationality is rooted in fact, but the lines of thought become exaggerated and are a product of grand delusions so that what starts as rational becomes irrational). Algernon, in this production, is taken over by his emotions and his energetic zeal. However, as an almost antirationalist, Algernon is ultimately rewarded by being able to marry Cecily. On the other hand, in this production, Jack's monotone graveness almost suggests that Jack is without emotions, that his reasoning behind being dutiful (for Cecily's sake) has stripped him of feeling (and all signs of being a dandy). To go back to what I said about the tension between fact and idea/concept in this play, this production shows the very tension that one normally sees between Algernon/Jack and Lady Bracknell is, instead, all bottled up inside of Jack, himself. Jack envisions himself as (the idea/concept of) Ernest, but his character is also fully earnest (as an observable, empirical fact). Therefore, Algernon and Lady Bracknell become mediated in Jack, who gets what he wants (i.e., Gwendolen) at the end. However, because Jack, very frankly, looks miserable most of the time (through gesture and vocal tone), the audience does not want to side with him (and what he says he desires, even though his desires are desirable to the audience). Algernon and, even, Lady Bracknell are much more fun to be around: given the two, however, one is always going to choose Algernon. And thus, the audience is left with Algernon, the one character who only strives toward (acts like) the ideal of being Ernest, but is, even to the end of the play, not ever factually Ernest (until presumably after the play is over and he will be christened Ernest). By allying themselves with Algernon, the tenets of Hegelian idealism and the denouncement of (the materialism of) fact, ultimately, are preferable for the audience.

In order to discuss Wilde's engagement with his political and philosophical era, it is first necessary to establish how these two plays are read through the idea of *insincere performances* (which must be theorized first before I do anything else). Once this idea is explored in an *explication de texte,* only then, I can turn at the end of this chapter back to the plays' political and philosophical debates.

Insincere Performances and "Bad Faith"

In order to develop the idea of "insincere performances," it is wise to start with the known, though heavily debated, concept of "performance." For this purpose, I am going to rely on just one definition: Richard Bauman's definition of performance. This limitation is based on four criteria. (1) Bauman's definition is well circulated throughout performance studies and is the basis for many other definitions. (2) By using one definition, though it does not reflect the complexity of the term, it is possible to establish a clear path to argue about insincere performances. (3) This chapter does not attempt to explore the many variegated lines of the contested term *performance.* (4) Bauman's idea of consciousness of doubleness parallels with the doubleness established by Sartre's idea of "bad faith," a concept on which I base my understanding of insincere performances.

Stated perhaps the most succinctly by Marvin Carlson, Bauman argues in the *International Encyclopedia of Communications* that "all performance involves a consciousness of doubleness, according to which the actual execution of an action is placed in mental comparison with a potential, an ideal, or a remembered original model of that action."[33] Important, as well, is the idea that "performance is always performance *for* someone."[34] In this sense, the actor that performs for an audience is doubly aware of the fact that they are performing and performing for someone.

In some sense, though, Bauman's definition of performance was already discussed many years earlier, in a different context, by Sartre in his famous chapter, "Bad Faith," in *Being and Nothingness*. Sartre's idea of "bad faith," which has also been nicely translated as "self-deception" in Walter Kaufman's influential text, *Existentialism: From Dostoevsky to Sartre*, has remained foundational to existentialism, but has yet to find its way into assessments of performance studies. I argue here that *insincere performance is the performance of "bad faith."* "Bad faith" is the situation in which a person lies to him or herself.[35] "Bad faith" is not lying in general, since "the essence of the lie implies in fact that the liar actually is in complete possession of the truth to which he is hiding."[36] In the act of lying, a liar knows he or she is not telling the truth. However, with bad faith, "the one who practices bad faith is hiding a displeasing truth or presenting as truth a pleasing untruth."[37] In short, the act of bad faith is self-deception where the person buys into his or her own lie. Any objection to comparing Bauman's performers who are aware that they are performing with people practicing self-deception, who may seem to be unaware of the doubleness, is addressed by the existential dilemma that Sartre addresses. In order to hide the displeasing truth or present a pleasing untruth, the person acting in "bad faith" must be conscious of the truth, "*in order* to conceal it more carefully."[38] The existential dilemma comes in when it is understood that a person must be in "good faith" simultaneously, as one must be conscious of one's bad faith in order to lie to oneself or to possess "bad faith."

Robert J. Yanal, probably unintentionally (given the fact that he wrote his essay on philosophy), brings the idea of "bad faith"/"self-deception" directly into conversation with the theatre. In his article entitled "Self-Deception and the Experience of Fiction," Yanal argues that the same trick of the mind that goes into self-deception enables fiction: "the willing suspension of disbelief."[39] Given that this statement applies most especially to the theatre, in this sense, then, both an actor and, especially, an audience must be in "bad faith" in order to watch a play. This understanding of "bad faith" illuminates "performance," as understood by Bauman, but in a sense it fails to take into account the doubleness that both Bauman and Sartre see in the act of acting.

Sartre gives an example of a waiter in a café to demonstrate the idea of "bad faith." Sartre paints a picture of a waiter whose "movement is quick and forward...chaining his movements as if they were mechanisms" in order to present himself as "some kind of automaton."[40] Sartre explains that

> ...he is playing at *being* a waiter in a café. There is nothing there to surprise us. The game is a kind of marking out and investigation. The child plays with his body in order to explore it, to take inventory of it; the waiter in the café plays with his condition in order to *realize* it.[41]

Much like Bauman's definition, there is an ideal that one is striving toward in performance. The waiter strives at being the archetypal waiter. However, Sartre takes this one step further and introduces the idea of "bad faith" into the performance:

> And it is precisely this person *who I have to be* (if I am the waiter in question) and who I am not. It is not that I do not wish to be this person or that I want this person to be different. But rather there is no common measure between his being and mine. It is a "representation" for others and for myself, which means that I can be he only in representation. But if I represent myself as him, I am not he...I can not be he, I can only play *at being* him...I am a waiter in the mode of *being what I am not*.[42]

Here, too, we see the idea of the consciousness of doubleness that the "representation" is "for others and for myself." But such a representation opens up the divide between the person and who or what he or she is representing. In this sense, a performance of "bad faith" is an insincere performance. The discussion of performing in "bad faith" opens up the idea of self-aware acting. The actor in "bad faith" is in constant awareness of "being what I am not." In this sense, Salome, Algernon, and Jack perform in "bad faith," in that as they enact their dual identities they have the awareness of "being what I am not."

To this end, I will examine three observations beginning with *Earnest*. (1) Algernon and Jack each have two named identities and the audience is fully aware of their double roles as they change locations. (2) In Algernon and Jack's admittance to the art of bunburying, the audience also becomes aware of Algernon and Jack's self-awareness of their acting. (3) Algernon and Jack are only "Algernon" and "Jack" in certain moments, at certain times, around certain company, and in certain places. In short, there is a conscious and self-aware divide between Algernon and Jack and their respective alter egos. The question that *Earnest* asks is, what is the difference between performing in earnest and performing insincerely (in "bad faith")? In a sense, this is the same question that *Salome* asks. My reading of *Salome* also relies on three observations about this serious rather than comedic/farcical drama. (1) Salome performs her own version of bunburying, moving between the realms of inside-the-palace and outside-the-palace. (2) In this sense, her identity also changes with the change of location. (3) Salome is self-aware of her different roles/selves. Ultimately, both these plays examine the performance of *being* or *not being*. The characters' "performances" and the "gaze" are pivotal to understanding their dramatic message.

THE IMPORTANCE OF BEING EARNEST

In considering one of the foundational quotes of performance studies from Johan Huizinga's *Homo Ludens,* who states that "all play means something,"[43] it, then, follows to turn to the opening scene of *Earnest*. The play begins in Algernon's flat, a space that is described as being *"luxuriously and artistically furnished."*[44] This description of the space immediately gives the reader a sense of Algernon's tastes. Though moneyed, or apparently so, Algernon also has an eye for art. This is important a moment later when we find out that Algernon is playing the piano. Not just someone who appreciates art, but someone who makes art himself, Algernon has an original take on playing the piano. When given the opportunity to perform on the piano, Algernon does not follow the prescribed notes:

ALGERNON: Did you hear what I was playing, Lane?
LANE: I didn't think it polite to listen, sir.
ALGERNON: I'm sorry for that, for your sake. I don't play accurately—any one can play accurately—but I play with wonderful expression. As far as the piano is concerned, sentiment is my forte. I keep science for Life.[45]

Though Algernon's line "I don't play accurately—any one can play accurately" is probably just a witty excuse to say he does not play well (and functions as a slight-of-hand to distract the audience and make the audience think his wit outpaces his piano playing ability), one has to consider the fact that maybe accuracy in art is not the most important thing: rather a "wonderful expression" may be more important than the details. This is a nod to Romanticism.

The decoration of the flat also curiously begs the question: for whom is Algernon decorating his flat? He may have an eye for art, himself, but is the art for him, or for the guest? *Who is Algernon's audience?* is another way of putting the question. This notion that Algernon might present a different lens through which others can view him is repeated in his words, in the question Algernon asks Lane: "Did you hear what I was playing, Lane?" Algernon is very aware of an outside listener and how his playing is coming across to others. Algernon also expresses sorrow for the fact that Lane was not listening, "for [Lane's] sake." But instead of stopping at that when Lane said he "didn't think it polite to listen," Algernon feels compelled to craft an image of how he wants his playing to come across. But how is the audience to take in this poor playing and Algernon's witty reframing of his piano playing abilities? Of course, as a function of being in the audience, it is only "polite to listen." Not listening to Algernon playing the piano would break the pact that is implicitly made by the audience member upon entering the theatre. Thus, the audience is now at odds with Algernon's perceived audience in the world of the play. Whereas Lane implicitly does not want to listen to Algernon playing the piano, in a sense, the audience has come to the theatre to take in the whole play (and that includes Algernon's piano playing). Thus at the onset of the play, with both how Algernon decorates his flat and how he plays the piano, we have a sense how competent Algernon is at self-deception. Like the decoration of his flat, which both alerts others as well as himself to his artistic nature, Algernon, in the face of playing the piano poorly, wants to see himself (and be seen) as artistic. Thus, Algernon rationalizes his inaccuracies and his lack of ability as justified by artistic license.

This idea that "wonderful expression" and "sentiment" are more important than accurate performance or portrayals fits with how Wilde's characters speak. Jacqueline Vanhoutte gives a similar assessment of the characters in Wilde's *Salome*: "In *Salome* and *The Importance of Being Earnest*, the characters are mere mouthpieces for the language: everyone in *Earnest* is a vehicle for wittiness... Wilde does not attempt to differentiate characters by their language: the plays' languages remain uniform, smooth, and more potent than the speakers themselves."[46] In some ways, all of the characters speak in "wonderful expression." However, although witticism was attributed to Wilde himself, there is a sense that Algernon should have a split personality when it comes to art and life, and thus, his speech should adjust to that fact. In playing the piano, "sentiment is [his] forte." Yet Algernon "keep[s] science for Life." One consequently would expect a much more dry, scientific tone and humor in Algernon's normal conversations than we see. But we do not encounter any somber tones from Algernon throughout the play. This may mean one of two things. Either (1) Algernon is lying to himself, or (2) Algernon does not *know himself*.

It is fruitful to examine the line "sentiment is my forte" to unravel this quandary. The important word here is "forte." Of course, in the most basic sense, this line reads, sentiment is my specialty/strength. But as a term in music, "forte" alerts the player to play loudly. And when marked *forté*, the notes in a particular passage should all be relatively played at the same loudness. This could be read in the almost monotone, mono-loudness reading that Vanhoutte attributes to the characters of *Salome* and *Earnest*. But there exists another way to read this line. Algernon's take on playing "forté" is to play, rather, with "sentiment." Being loud is playing with "wonderful expression."

In *Earnest*, Wilde creates a character/character-within-the-character dichotomy. Therefore, it is no wonder that these dual identities in *Earnest* have previously been described by Clifton Snider though the trope of the trickster. Taking the idea of the trickster from the Jungian tradition of synchronicity, Snider defines the trickster, most particularly in his article, as a character who can traverse boundaries.[47] This furthers the idea that Algernon and Jack are liminal characters. As queer theory suggests, Algernon and Jack move between the roles of heterosexuality and homosexuality through the role of the dandy. Especially given the details of Wilde's biography, there exists a high level of self-deception when one plays it straight. But although this reading is suggestive, Lalonde sees this dandy dual identity as thoroughly heterosexual through the performance of class and sexuality:

> ...both Algernon and Jack in Earnest display heterosexual desire. If anything, there is the suggestion that Algernon might be promiscuously heterosexual in spite of his effeminacy... Wilde demonstrates how the effeminacy of the dandy signifies in a host of ways—how it is as much a performance of class as it is potentially a performance of sexuality.[48]

The performance of class (and, of course, sexuality) in *Earnest* raises a tangential, but important, parallel to Bertolt Brecht's *The Good Person of Szechwan*.

The idea of performance in this play, especially insincere performance, specifically relates to Brechtian themes found in Brecht's *The Good Person of Szechwan*. To create a quick but slightly different parallel, like Algernon, who is Bunbury in town, away from the city, Shui Ta, the masculine alter ego of Shen Teh in Brecht's play, comes to town due to economic and class pressures. The creation of a hyper-masculine alter ego that allows the characters to get what they want is common to both; for example, Algernon asks Lane to "put up [his] dress clothes, [his] smoking jacket, and all the Bunbury suits...,"[49] and Shen Teh dresses like a man. But there is a marked difference between these two plays. Shui Ta, the alter ego, is antithetical to Shen Teh's real personality. Shui Ta is ruthless and defiant, unlike the passive and submissive Shen Teh. However, in *Earnest*, for both Algernon and Jack, their alter egos (i.e., Bunbury and Ernest) are their true selves and "Algernon" and "Jack" are Societal archetypes. When both characters are bunburying—when they are being Ernest—they want to marry. Though the two differ in this respect—that is, the ego/alter ego dichotomy is opposite—the two plays both comment on the need for an individual to create two antithetical selves in order to please a stifling society.

The problem in *Earnest* (and later in *Salome*), then, is that does the audience's perception of Algernon and Jack's (and Salome's) different selves constitute a truthful reality, or do their actions, given their insincere performances, somehow taint the amalgamation of appearances into a unified Absolute truth? Therefore, is truth something ever out of our reach in these plays? These two questions get to the very heart of the play and the tension present between idealism and materialism (and thus these questions will be raised again later).

If we take into account Fforde's description of the Right and the Left, in Gwendolen's statement, "We live... in an age of ideals," we understand the Right's attempt at *striving* for individual virtue, which, if reached, would create an ideal "gentleman," and the Left's notion of an ideal society. The notion of "ideal" is rooted in *desire*. An "ideal" is a *desirable idea* to be striven for in hopes that the idea becomes reality. Wilde complicates this notion of idea and ideal in Bunburying. Bunburying alleviates societal desire (i.e., that individuals should strive to be virtuous gentlemen), desires not shared by the individual, and enables the creation of a societally undesirable, but individually advantageous idea (i.e., a wicked/sick person, almost the opposite of an ideal, virtuous gentleman):

> *JACK*: ... When one is placed in the position of guardian, one has to adopt a very high moral tone on all subjects. It's one's duty to do so. And as a high moral tone can hardly be said to conduce very much either to one's health or one's happiness, in order to get up to town I have always pretended to have a younger brother of the name of Ernest, who lives in the Albany, and gets into the most dreadful scrapes. That, my dear Algy, is the whole truth pure and simple.
> *ALGERNON*: The truth is rarely pure and never simple...[50]

Jack brings up the question of happiness. He assumes his unhappiness comes from "adopting a high moral tone" (with the understanding that that simply is not fun, relaxing, etc.). Algy, speaking here presumably for Wilde, recognizes the complexity of the situation: desire and happiness are on two different planes (i.e., fulfilling desire does not necessarily bring happiness).

Jack and Algy's happiness is only assured at the very end of the play, not necessarily because they are getting married (i.e., what they desire), but only when who they are (ontologically) matches who they are perceived to be (epistemologically, both by themselves and by an audience). In other words, being Ernest/earnest is the unification of splintered selves into an ontologically and epistemologically coherent whole. However, of course, in this case, a unified whole comes at the expense of shedding parts of the self: selves that either contradict or do not make a tidy whole. While happiness may be gained, it must be remembered that there is still something lost.

In seeing two diametrically opposed selves, the play, again, alienates and "allows us to recognize its subject, but at the same time makes it seem unfamiliar." The audience member sees the need for an individual performance based upon context. *When I am with my aunt, for example, particular to this play, versus my friend, I act and speak differently,* the audience member thinks. Though *Earnest* was not an originally historically relative play (though it is now), *Earnest* is a *societally and situationally relative play*: the audience asks itself, how would I act, "if I had lived under those circumstances?" [51] *What if I moved in those social circles? What if I had no prestigious lineage? What if I was unhappy with my social circle?*

Returning to *Earnest* and an earlier point, what becomes peculiar is that although Algernon and Jack occupy two distinct social circles (one in the city and one in town), and thus one would expect a degree of assimilation or passing in each respective circle, their language remains constant and unchanged. I think what this suggests is that although Algernon and Jack play two characters, they are unable to fully adapt to either character, as their speech pattern and choice of language gives them away. And furthermore, these two characters become indistinguishable from each other by their wit. The effect is twofold: (1) the two are inept at social and situational performances from the eyes of the audience, despite their supposed skill at bunburying, and/or (2) the stress of having to perform for two different audiences makes them retreat into their comfort zone—wit and humor, which are well-known defense mechanisms to handle uncomfortable situations. Adolf Barth argues that "Whenever these figures are made to take off their 'shallow masks of manners,' it is not deep characters we see. Rather, the author emerges signalizing the evasive mockery and ironic artificiality of the dramatic construct."[52] The effect, I argue, is that Algernon and Jack's speech allows the audience to see through the artifice of the theatre and see Algernon and Jack's "sentiment" of the two characters each plays.

What we have in Jack and Algernon are two characters who are forced to split their personalities in order to lead the life that they want. The tragedy of this is that they are never able to *be* themselves. In the case of *The Good Person of Szechwan,* Shen Teh at least has the comfort of being who she is, while necessity forces her to create an alter ego, Shui Ta. However, in *Earnest,* Algernon and Jack constantly live in "bad faith." On one hand, when Jack is in the country, he is himself, but "has to adopt a very high moral tone on all subjects."[53] In this sense, when he is Jack, he is insincerely performing what he is not. On the other hand, when in the city, Jack exposes his true feelings about a marriage to Gwendolen. However, Jack is Ernest there, someone who he is not. Thus, in both cases, Jack is being what he is not. Likewise Algernon, when he is in the city, for the sake of societal appearances, must shun marriage. But the first glimpse of Cecily makes Bunbury, Algernon's alter ego, want to marry. So again, in both cases, Algernon is being what he is not. He enacts an insincere performance. He is living in "bad faith."

When Jack explains to Algernon how he is placed in the role of guardian, he explains that it is his "duty" to take a high moral tone. However, this "duty" he feels is at odds with his own happiness: "...a high moral tone can hardly be said to conduce very much to either one's health or one's happiness..."[54] Thus sadly, he has to create an alter ego, Ernest, to appease his desires and happiness. Algernon sums up the play thusly, "My dear fellow, it isn't easy to be anything nowadays."[55] The reason that being anything is difficult is that the society that Algernon and Jack belong to lives in "bad faith." But what makes this "bad faith" is that Algernon is fully aware of how difficult it is "to be."

A Return to Philosophy

One of the reasons why Algernon is fully aware of how difficult it is "to be" is that he is also fully aware of how difficult it is *not to be*. Here, Wilde is echoing his contemporary philosophical debates about solving the problem between Being and Not-Being. In terms of Wilde's synthesis of Wallace and Jowett and other Hegelian idealists, truth is presented through the dialectic of Being and Not-Being. Speaking about Sartre's previously mentioned waiter, Joseph S. Catalano argues, "I take Sartre's point to be that the very condition for the possibility of not-being a waiter is created simultaneously with the fact of being a waiter..."[56] The result, as Catalano suggests, is that when in bad faith, one hides from the responsibility to either choose/sustain or change one's lifestyle.[57] This is the primary predicament of the play: Algernon, and Jack presumably before the time of the play, both bunbury in order to avoid their responsibilities of choosing/sustaining their dual lifestyles or changing their lifestyles; thus they live in bad faith/self-deception.

This performance of self-deception is all that more complex when a witness is added to the picture. Timothy Chambers discusses this aspect of self-deception in a book review of George Yancy's *Black Bodies, White Gaze: The Continuing Significance of Race*. Chambers notes how a witness can be both detrimental and good for someone living in bad faith:

> Sartre notoriously defined hell as other people, and the gaze is a pivotal reason why. Others inspect my behaviour, but since they're unable to introspect my subjectivity, their judgements of me are bound to be starker, harsher, than my self-evaluations. Sometimes, this is to the good, as when an interlocutor can confront my self-deception (*mauvaise foi*) and corner me into taking responsibility.[58]

In *The Importance of Being Earnest,* the gaze does not just come from the audience, but is directed at the characters from the other characters in the play. The question then becomes, given that there is a gaze upon Algernon and Jack, how is it that Jack and, especially, Algernon do not confront their performances of self-deception? The answer to this is that, particularly, Algernon is in a position of power where he can deflect the gaze.

Algernon is a bachelor in a privileged position; he employs someone beneath him, Lane; and he has no living parents. Also, Algernon has a desirable object: Gwendolen. Therefore, even though Algernon tells Jack about his own bunburying, Jack has no power of persuasion to force Algernon to confront his insincere performance. Jack wants what Algernon can withhold from him (Gwendolen). On the other hand, when Jack is caught in his act of bunburying by Algernon, Jack *now* declares that he has had enough with it and wants to kill off Ernest.

But their gaze is not just directed upon each other. Aunt Augusta suspends her disbelief numerous times when Algernon says that there were no cucumbers at the market or when Aunt Augusta rightly observes that Bunbury is constantly sick. With no pressure from parents to physically and symbolically remind Algernon of familial obligations, Algernon is able to deflect the gaze of guilt and, thus, he is not forced to confront his insincere performance.

It is not a gaze that forces, at least, Algernon to confront his insincere performance. What forces Algernon into facing the responsibility of changing his lifestyle, to look at it from Catalano's perspective, are Algernon's own desires. Given that it is difficult to be a bachelor because Algernon and Jack have to enact an insincere performance, it is just as difficult for Algernon and Jack to be married. Their insincere performances of bunburying force them to lie to themselves about how terrible marriage is and, thus, they do not know themselves. However, at the first glimmer of hope of a married life, both characters need to be, both literally and figuratively, Ernest/earnest with themselves.

Salome

The seeming impetus for Algernon and Jack's bunburying comes from the pressures of *being looked at*. Of course, the divided selves that the two create are imprecise images of themselves: neither half is true and neither half is false. The gaze inward, then, is next to impossible when one is simultaneously *being* and *not being* him or herself. Thus, although Algy and Jack do benefit by killing off their bunburying other half, in a sense, they still have to kill off part of themselves to be happy, if one can argue that they are happy at the end of the play. Understanding Salome as a bunburyer herself brings these two plays into a dialogue. Everyone, including the audience, is looking at Salome. However, still she seems to be elusive. What I argue here is that Salome splits herself, revealing different parts of herself in different situations depending upon the differing gazes. Salome is a canny bunburyer: however, only Salome bunburys (splits in two) to escape the gaze of others in order to preserve parts of herself.

The "gaze" is not an uncommon theme when it comes to the scholarship surrounding *Salome*. Two articles, both published in 1998, examine the gaze in *Salome* in great detail. Forest Pyle takes meaning out of the Iokanaan's line, "the lust of her eyes," by arguing that the gaze is thematized and theatricalized in *Salome*.[59] Especially where Herod's gaze upon Salome is concerned, Pyle suggests that the language of the play is less in the domain of meaning and more in the domain of doing, of performance and effect.[60] Similarly, given that opera is usually thought of in the aural realm, Linda Hutcheon and Michael Hutcheon argue that in Strauss' *Salome,* the verbal, the visual, and the aural are thematized.[61] When Salome dances, Hutcheon and Hutcheon argue, the gaze of the audience creates a conflation of verbal, visual, and musical arts, as Salome does not sing, but Salome's dance is supported by the orchestra for ten minutes.[62] What particularly interests me in these two articles is that these scholars see the effects of performance on the play and opera. Whereas, for example, Pyle admirably examines how the gaze draws, in performance, the audience's attention to gender politics,[63] what is novel in his assessment is understanding the gaze in *Salome,* not just in performance, but in relation to its performative nature as understood in performance studies. More specifically, Salome's self-awareness when confronted by the gaze of Herod and the Court, turns, especially, the "Dance of the Seven Veils" into an *insincere performance:* Salome performs "bad faith" much like when Algernon and Jack do when they bunbury.

Salome's first lines in the play reveal the impossible predicament of *being Salome:* "I will not stay. I cannot stay. Why does the Tetrarch look at me all the while with his mole's eye under his shaking eyelids?"[64] Presumably, the third line, which discusses Herod's gaze upon Salome, explains the fact why Salome "will not" and "cannot stay." The idea of her staying or leaving because of a gaze raises four points. (1) Implied in the idea of *stay*—"To cease moving, halt"[65]—is the idea that staying is a temporary state. "Moving" is the activity that is stopped. For Salome, then, her home—the palace—is a place where *she* ceased moving (*she* "cannot stay"); the palace, itself, is also a temporary home. In a metaphoric sense, Salome does not belong in the palace. The palace is a holding ground both for herself and for her movement. In this sense, staying in the palace is a liminal act for a liminal character, stuck in an in-between. However, outside of the palace, in scenes with The Young Syrian, we recognize that Salome does not belong there either, as nobody is her equal. (2) If Salome leaves the palace, then, Salome will no longer live in a place designed to house a princess. Her very stay at the palace implies her royalty. However, the temporariness of the stay suggests that it is possible that once she leaves the palace, so too does an element of her royalty leave her (as her departure would imply a disownership of the King and Queen). (3) Whether or not she stays or leaves, Salome's identity is couched in her location: either place, a part of Salome does not exist (whether her ability to move or her birthright as a princess). (4) The "gaze" of Herod turns Salome into a commoner: as the *object* of his gaze, Salome becomes his *subject*. This is a paradoxical, liminal state for Salome. What all four of these points have in common is that Salome is a paradox. Just as Algernon and Jack cannot be themselves, Salome has no ability *to be Salome*.

The impossibility of *being Salome* highlights the fact as to why Salome is always described "like" something.[66] Just like Salome's "stay" in the palace denotes her temporary state, *being like* something, instead of *being* something displays the inexactitude of *being Salome*. However, there is one time that Salome is defined with certainty: Salome introduces herself to Iokanaan, "I am Salome, daughter of Herodias, Princess of Judea."[67] (Note the fact that Herod has nothing to do with her identity in this pronouncement.) The significance of this introduction lies in the fact that Iokanaan is the prophet, who metaphorically sees all, but does not know it is Salome until she states it herself. Metaphorically, it is the prophet who sees, but in this case, he is blind to her identity. Thus, Salome only feels comfortable with who she is (as she states it above with exactitude) when a person (in this case, Iokanaan) does not see or gaze upon her *as Salome*. Salome, then, is in an awful predicament. She is only herself, Salome (to herself in "earnest"), when she is *not Salome* to others. Likewise, as long as remains "Salome" to others, she simultaneously is *not Salome in earnest*.

Salome's change of location, both inside and outside of the palace, is Salome's version of bunburying. Like Algernon and Jack, Salome is in a constant state of simultaneously "being" and "not being" while her location changes. In both instances, Salome remains the object of the gaze. However, outside of the palace, The Young Syrian is gazing, metaphorically, up at her, just as he gazes up at the moon, the object that Salome is "like." Similarly, inside of the palace, Herod gazes down at Salome as his subject. Confusion as to Salome's place abounds when she is inside. Salome is both commanded by Herod to dance, and she commands Herod to give her the head of Iokanaan. Likewise, Salome is addressed by Herod as "Salome" when asked to dance for the last time, "Dance, Salome, dance for me,"[68] but when Herod looks back down at Salome at the end of the play from midway up the stairs, he says, "Kill that woman!"[69] No matter her location, for Salome, it is just as difficult "to be" as "not to be." It is in the Dance of the Seven Veils that Salome performs in "bad faith." For all of the numerous reasons explained above, when Salome acts *as Salome* for others (for Salome is addressed as "Salome" by Herod), she is not true to herself and thus she is performing in "bad faith."

When Herod calls her "that woman" (as opposed to "Salome"), there is a parallel to when Iokanaan does not recognize Salome, for Wilde makes a suggestion through the stage directions that Salome is, in fact, herself at this precarious moment. In the stage directions, Wilde writes that the soldiers kill *"Salome, daughter of Herodias, Princess of Judea."*[70] This references back to Salome's own pronouncement of who she is when she first meets Iokanaan. It is in her moment of death, when Herod no longer sees her as "Salome," that Wilde suggests that Salome is, again, herself and free of Herod in terms of her identity. And thus, it is impossible *to be Salome:* for only in death is Salome herself, as suggested by Wilde's stage directions.

Though I have established a parallel between two highly disparate plays through the idea of insincere performance, why did Oscar Wilde specifically choose the Salome story to examine the plight of performing in "bad faith"? I think the clue can be found in Salome's *presence* in the Bible. Salome both exists and does not exist in the Bible. Because Salome is unnamed in the Bible, she is indefinite and amorphous. However, given the Zen Buddhist idea that once you name something you kill it, Salome is also full of possibilities since she is unnamed. Therefore, when Herod proclaims, "Kill that woman!" Herod may have killed the woman, but he did not kill the idea. In a similar sense, while in *Earnest,* who Algy and Jack are at the end of the play mirrors who they are perceived to be, in *Salome,* the pronouncement of "Kill that woman!" suggests that by the end of the play who Salome is still does not match how she is perceived. And, in this way, *Salome* is a tragedy. However, by the grace of the playwright's pen in the final stage directions—"*Salome, daughter of Herodias, Princess of Judea*"—Wilde shows that he both *perceives* and *knows* Salome as one and the same person (and, thus, the audience does, as well). In this sense, Salome, her story, and her paradox (the same paradoxes shared by the masses in Wilde's society) live on and will be explored forever.

Conclusion: *Insincere Performance* as Philosophical and Political Commentary

There is a problem present with *insincere performances* yet to be discussed. If we return to the Actor-Audience relationship, we soon realize that there is at least some awareness of the fact that this is a performance for the "actor" (e.g., Algernon, Jack, and Salome). However, the audience (Lady Bracknell, Gwendolen, Cecily, Herod, the Young Syrian, etc.), on the other hand, is unaware that this is a performance. In *insincere performances,* then, the actor performs *for* the audience (just as in *performance*). However, in these instances, the audience does not realize that he/she/they constitute(s) an audience.

Given the intentionality of the character and the unawareness of the audience, the splitting of each character into two separate but related selves poses an epistemological problem. To return to what I discussed earlier regarding Bradley's view of Absolute Idealism, Bradley sees reality (the Absolute) as the sum total of all appearances. These appearances are the finite parts (perspectives, in a sense) of an Absolute whole (i.e., reality). Now in a different context, I am going to repeat a question that I posed earlier that is central to the play: does the audience's perception of Algernon and Jack's (and Salome's) different selves constitute a truthful reality, or do their actions, given their insincere performances, somehow taint the amalgamation of appearances into a unified Absolute truth? This question raises the possibility that truth is something always out of our reach. That is, some of the appearances are "true" (to the point where the sum total of these types of "true" appearances constitute an Absolute reality), but others are "false" (in that the performance of "bad faith" does not accurately help the audience understand any normal sense of truth).

Furthermore, the unawareness of the audience gives the upper hand to the "actors." This opens up a space for the "actors" to subvert the hegemony and present truth in such a way that is advantageous to themselves. In a sense, Wilde moves past the idealism/materialism debate altogether and Wilde anticipates the Foucauldian idea of truth that is wrapped up in power relations. However, *Earnest* and *Salome* present two different forms of power. *Salome*, set in Biblical Palestine, represents Foucault's idea of a top-down power structure, where King Herod doles out regulations to his subjects. It is in this society that Salome, no matter how subversive her insincere performance is, cannot affect any change and she finds herself the victim of Herod's whims. Despite her privileged position in its society, power is located in one place (Herod), and any deviation of the regulations that Herod's power sets forth, creates something of a revolt. Given Herod's absolute power, revolts can be quashed. *Earnest,* on the other hand, constitutes a Foucauldian network of power, where Algernon and Jack use the ideals of the hegemony to undermine it in order to make that hegemony, which they want to enter, into something more palatable for them.

The juxtaposition of these two plays, with *Salome* being written first, almost suggests to the audience that Wilde is showing that there is an opportunity for subversive agency to create a Socialist state in the form that Wilde put forth. In a sense, Wilde is trying to show how, with Salome, she is someone who operates similarly to Algernon and Jack, yet the power structure in her society did not allow for any type of societal reorganization. On the other hand, if the audience member then sees *Earnest,* then he or she will see a contemporary society where subversive agency is possible. *Earnest* when juxtaposed against *Salome* becomes a call to arms for Wilde's own society. Algernon represents the model citizen of Wilde's ideal Socialist society who overcomes Lady Bracknell (who, bringing the Right's view to bear, represents the Right) and Jack (who, bring the Left's view to bear, is a product of his fortunate circumstances, as he was luckily adopted by a wealthy man).

To conclude, I want to examine the much-discussed subtitle of *The Importance of Being Earnest: A Trivial Comedy for Serious People.*

I believe that the phrase "trivial comedy" has received too much of the attention, while the phrase "for serious people" has not received enough. By focusing on "trivial comedy," one surmises that this is a comedy about the trivial, and how this play is commonly produced can speak to this reading of the subtitle. However, if the focus is on the phrase "for serious people," then the subtitle can mean *for serious people, this comedy is trivial*. In a sense, serious people might brush this off as trivial because, since this is also incisively poking fun at the serious, the serious people in the audience would psychologically want to brush off their perceived faults as something trivial, without consequence.

If this is a "Trivial Comedy for Serious People," what, then, is this play for people who are not serious? Though Wilde is a serious intellectual, it is hard to call Wilde, himself, serious. Can we then say that this (playing off of the subtitle) is *a serious play for unserious people*? And if that is the case, I argue that we have taken ourselves way too seriously in regard to this play: by being "serious" in producing this play, we have missed the play's intellectual and philosophical seriousness. And the great irony is that we have turned our "gaze" on the triviality of the Victorian society in the play, but by doing so, we have ignored both "gazing" at ourselves (to understand where we fall the serious-trivial spectrum in order to produce the play and understanding ourselves) and the seriousness and implications of the "gaze" in *Earnest*.

Acknowledgments

I wish to thank Timothy Chambers of the Philosophy Department at the University of Hartford for reading an earlier draft of this chapter, providing useful feedback, and ensuring that my philosophical arguments are well founded based upon current, scholarly philosophical conversations. An earlier and shorter version of this chapter, with a different emphasis (i.e., the emphasis was only on insincere performances and had nothing to do with the epistemological debate that is found in this chapter), was previously published: Michael Y. Bennett, "A Wilde Performance: Bunburying and 'Bad Faith' in *The Importance of Being Earnest* and *Salome*," *Refiguring Oscar Wilde's* Salome, ed. Michael Y. Bennett (Amsterdam: Rodopi, 2011) 167–181.

CHAPTER 2

AFTER THE GREAT WAR: CONTEXTUALIZING THE *SELF* IN ITALY AND *SIX CHARACTERS IN SEARCH OF AN AUTHOR*

> I can't see...
> —Opening line of *Six Characters in Search of an Author*[1]

LUIGI PIRANDELLO'S *Six Characters in Search of an Author* (1921) permanently changed the face and possibilities of theatre. The premiere of this play ruptured the history of the theatre: this constituted a "before" and an "after" moment. Starting with Ibsen and the theatrical realism that he gave rise to, playwrights put the "fourth wall" *behind* the audience: the audience, though invisible to the characters, was in the "room" with the characters. Pirandello, on the other hand, moved the "fourth wall" *in front of* the audience: the audience could not ignore the fact that a play is a theatrical event. Pirandello's meta-theatrical move, though the meta- in theatre had its traces back at least to the Senecan "aside," was certainly jarring given the, now (in 1921), well-established conventions of theatrical realism.

Looking solely at the history of the theatre, Pirandello's play was a glaring departure from theatrical realism. However, if the play is contextualized in its political, social, artistic, intellectual, and philosophical history, it is thoroughly a product of its time (though universal in its epistemological quest). In a world still in shock over the Great War, I argue that the meta-theatrics forced the audience to not only reexamine the "idealism" of the theatre and weigh it against a type of theatrical "pragmatism," but by using the meta-theatrical to highlight the differences and similarities in the actor/character/audience member, Pirandello forced the audience to reexamine the *self* in the context of the debate between philosophical idealism and pragmatism. The question that Pirandello poses in *Six Characters in Search of an Author* is, do we have to "see" the self to *know* the self?

THE DAWNING OF THE INTERWAR CRISIS

The hope that followed the end of "the war to end all wars" was short lived and a period of instability soon followed. The Treaty of Versailles in June 1919 sought international peace, but the difficulty of this accomplishment became awfully apparent.[2] As R. J. Overy suggests, social unrest, economic stagnation, and international political conflict weighed heavily against the hopes for peace abroad and the stability at home. This new, post-1918 reality contrasted so greatly with the world before the Great War that the *belle époque* "seemed rosier than ever now that it was lost." This is why, in part, Overy argues—following the line first established by Edward Hallett Carr in his seminal work, *The Twenty Years' Crisis*—that the interwar crisis was different from previous crises, in that this was the first *self-aware* crisis where populations were confronted with "an age of unstable transformation."[3] The transformation that occurred could be well demonstrated by looking at territorial maps around 1900 and 1920: one would notice large territorial empires run by hereditary monarchies (with the exception of France) around 1900; by 1920, only two empires—the British and the French—remained (though they were under increasing pressure from their territories for reform from nationalist groups).[4] Overy suggests that "the war did more than any other single event to reinforce the impression of crisis, of forces out of control, of a world lost for ever."[5] Overy suggests that for many people in most of the nineteenth century, Western civilization appeared to be something permanent and progressive; the Great War, then, propagated their disillusionment. The assumption that Western civilization was in crisis was reinforced by German philosopher Oswald Spengler's influential book, *Decline of the West* (1918), which was met by a receptive audience.[6]

Revolution was both a symptom and the result of this sense of crisis. The Russian Revolution was not an event confined to its own country. After the overthrow of the Tsarist regime in Russia, the Bolshevik uprising disturbed those in the West, a place full of social unrest (as four years of war created problems on the home fronts from inflation to food shortages to declining health).[7] Fearful of a left-wing takeover in Western countries, popular counterrevolutions were taking place. Specifically, in Italy, Benito Mussolini, ex-Socialist turned nationalist, set up the *Fasci di combattimento:* a group of veterans who attacked left-wing demonstrations, burned down Socialist offices, and threw strikers out of factories, all paid for by landlords and business people.[8] The Italian Fascist Party formed in 1921 as the violent counterrevolution brought frightened property owners and nationalists into the movement.[9] (Mussolini became prime minister in October 1922.)

It makes sense, to a degree, that revolution was the game of the day: life, for many Europeans, had changed vastly over the course of the Great War. First, there was move away from peasantry. This coincided with a massive move from rural to urban areas. Many peasants themselves were off fighting in the war, and meanwhile, farms, horses, and oxen were seized for the armies. On return, small farmers confronted new economic pressures, as the population grew and small farmers had to compete with cheap overseas imports that pushed down the price of food.[10] Second, the very shape of business was changing: from small businesses with one or two employees to factories. In the beginning of the century, small producers were still set up much like the guild system. The war changed this. First, the war industry favored large firms over small ones. And second, many of the tradesmen who worked in these small firms were drafted into the army, and with the shortage of raw materials and the import of mass-produced goods, the production of small firms was disrupted.[11] The end result was that cheap mass-produced goods from the United States or Japan pushed out many small-scale, handmade productions. This resulted in the consolidation of business to fewer and larger industry firms.

Despite its unevenness, industry grew ever-upward after 1918. However, the shape of the economy changed. Until 1914, with economies relying on the Gold Standard and the strength of the British economy (with their interest on keeping the world markets stable as Britain had imperial interests around the globe), the world had 30 years of virtual growth in industrial output and world trade. The war fundamentally changed the world's economy. The United States and Japan supplanted European export markets while the Europeans were fighting the war. And because European goods were not being made in the same large-scale manner that they were prior to the war, those countries that depended upon European goods had to start their own industrialization process and move to other suppliers. When European goods were finally being produced again, there was widespread overproduction, which caused prices to slump. All of this, along with the relatively poor performance of the British economy in the 1920s (British exports were down and, thus, Britain had less money to buy other nation's exports, greatly affecting the world economy), led to the undermining of the world economic structure that remained so stable before the war.[12]

The instability of the world economy—or at least a rupture of a before and an after moment—helped fuel the sense of crisis. Advances in science, most notably from Albert Einstein and his theories of relativity, "demonstrated clearly that the universe was behaving like 'an exploding grenade' and, as a consequence, that its life was finite."[13] David Cassidy discusses what the monumental discoveries in science meant to many people following the Great War:

> ...many feared that the triumph of relativity meant, by its very name, the decline of the old transcendent moral order and the triumph of universal "relativism" in every sphere of life—a gross misunderstanding and erroneous extension of relativity theory. If the basic "given" elements of nature where no longer absolute and independent of human observers, many reasoned, then neither were traditional meanings and beliefs in religion, ethics, and social ideology. Coming on the top of the upheavals over Darwinian evolution, science seemed to be telling the public—as it does to some

in the United States today—that cherished values and beliefs are a mere illusion.[14]

But it was not only on a cosmic scale that science was fundamentally shaping a view of crisis. Science altered how people thought of themselves. Though the main goal of psychoanalysis was therapeutic relief for the mentally ill, the expansion of psychoanalysis (both Freudian and many other schools that spawned in Freud's wake) created another scientific metaphor of crisis: that every individual was a divided self, simultaneously rational on the outside and one who houses uncontrollable and invisible psychological urges.[15]

As Modris Eksteins argues, the perceived decline of civilization led to refocusing on the self:

> As the war's meaning began to be enveloped in a fog of existential questioning, the integrity of the "real" world, the visible and ordered world, was undermined. As the war called into question the rational connection of the prewar world—the nexus, that is, of cause and effect—the meaning of civilization as tangible achievement was assaulted, as was the nineteenth-century view that all history represented progress. And as the external world collapsed in ruins, the only redoubt of integrity became the individual personality... As the past went down the drain, the *I* became all-important.[16]

This focus on the self went hand in hand with the founding of the Dada movement. Meeting in Zurich in 1915—most notably Hugo Ball, Richard Huelsenbeck, Hans Richter, Hars Arp, and Tristan Tzara—the Dada movement created an anti-art, whose only sense was nonsense.[17] The Dada movement best characterized what Overy said was the *modus operandi* of the age: "The order of the day was experiment and challenge."[18] Thus, the Dada movement was accompanied by movements in art, music, literature, and science: the European high art of conventional portraits and landscapes was supplanted by the creativity of Pablo Picasso and Wassily Kandinsky; Arnold Schoenberg revolutionized musical composition that would come to be the foundation of contrapuntal and atonal music; science produced the automobile and the airplane; and engineers and architects looked past bricks and tiles in favor of steel, concrete, and glass.[19]

All of the pressures on the world, both economically and psychologically, found themselves bottled up in Italy between the end of WWI and the ascension of Mussolini to prime minister in 1922. Before the war, Italy lagged far behind the other industrialized European nations in almost all categories: available materials, per capita gross national product, literacy rates, and health.[20] As a result, strikes, lockouts and social violence were on the rise in prewar Italy.[21] One of the causes for such turmoil was Italy's dramatic class differences.[22] Much of this had to do with Italy's long history of the "elite's nervousness about the masses."[23]

After the war, during the first year of "peace," Italy was in crisis (as was much of Europe): economically, socially, and politically. Without a clear "leader" of the Liberal elite (the ruling party throughout the war), other voices, most notably the Fascists, made their way into the national conversation.[24] The socialists were gaining power (i.e., seats) in government in the couple of years following the war, but the Socialist movement in Italy was quite divided in its direction.[25] The first big opposition group (to the socialists) that emerged in postwar Italy was organized political Catholicism (*Partito Popolare Italiano* [PPI]), which won a substantial number of seats in 1919, but which, too, was a party equally suffering from internal disputes.[26] The internal divisions among the Liberals and Catholics, and the great economic and social pressures that reached a boiling point after the war, allowed a new right to step in and denounce and attempt to liquidate what it saw as "Bolshevism."[27] This new Right, the *fasci*, clearly annunciated its enemy: socialism and those opposing the nationalistic view of Italy's war.[28] Right away, the Fascist movement, although still amorphous and solidifying what exactly it was between 1919 and when it became a party in 1921,

> ...did not hide or apologize for its social Darwinism and warmongering, its use of social and military terror and its fondness for pre-emptive assault...As early as 1920, Mussolini spoke in favour of "ethnic cleansing" in the Balkans...[29]

And with the lira tumbling (which made it hard for Italy to secure international credit) during the early months of 1920[30] and a spate of strikes that caused much social disorder for much of 1920,[31] *Il Duce* and the *fasci* soon found themselves in power.

ITALY'S PRAGMATISTS AND IDEALISTS

Italy and Mussolini's rise to power was not just due to economic pressures. The rise of fascism had deep connections to the philosophical debates between pragmatism and idealism throughout the first two decades of the century. While pragmatism supplanted idealism in much of the West, Italy, though it did have a brief movement of pragmatism, fell back on idealism. And this particular brand of Italian idealism provided much of the rationale for fascism. Pragmatism, which had its roots in the United States with Charles Sanders Peirce, William James, and John Dewey and migrated to England with F. C. S. Schiller as its main proponent, was a response to British Idealism (which, as a line of rationalism, put forth the general tenets of the existence of an Absolute reality that can only be understood fully through reason). Pragmatism's main argument is that if x is actually true, then x will work in reality: in other words, it is an empirical philosophy because ideas are only true if they can be verified by observation; ideas are not something that should remain in the realm of abstraction, but should be verifiable, or rather, the idea should work out in the real world. Pragmatism, however brief, had a life outside of the United States and England. H. S. Thayer begins his chapter on Italian pragmatism in *Meaning and Action: A Critical History of Pragmatism* with a story about James, the American pragmatist *par excellence,* and his visit to Rome:

> When James was attending the Fifth International Congress of Psychology in Rome in 1905, he met and conversed with a "little band of 'pragmatists.' " James was very much impressed. "It has," he wrote,
>
>> given me a certain new idea of the way in which truth ought to find its way into the world. The most interesting, and in fact genuinely edifying, part of my trip has been meeting this little *cénable,* who have taken my own writings, *entre autres, au grand sérieux.*
>
> Speaking of this "band," James remarked that they "publish the monthly Journal *Leonardo* at their own expense, and carry on a very serious philosophic movement, apparently really inspired by Schiller and myself."[32]

This "band" was made up of Giovanni Papini, Giuseppe Prezzolini, Giovanni Vailati, Mario Calderoni, and Giovanni Amendola.

The principal pragmatist in Italy was Papini, who argued for a pluralism that urged for complete involvement in collective or individual activity.[33] Action, then, was at the heart of Papini's pragmatism. Since Papini argues that reality is malleable, it is action that transforms reality to more fully realize our own ideals and desires: ideals, myths, and concepts are created for the purpose of molding reality.[34] Fundamentally an empiricist claim, Papini argues that reality, not thought, is what needs to be adapted through action to human interests.[35] Prezzolini was of the same ilk as Papini, and like Papini, a follower of Schiller. Prezzolini (like Schiller) vigorously attacked formal logic and logicians, as Prezzolini reasoned that "the better part of human thought is not to be found in logic, and the best use of language is not to serve thought but the will."[36]

This pragmatist movement in Italy, however, really only lasted about the first ten years of the century. Thayer lists the numerous reasons why this flourishing movement ended so quickly: the Church was suspicious of Modernism (which had some alliance with pragmatism); the idealism of Benedetto Croce and Giovanni Gentile became increasingly influential; the philosophic dissension between "magical" and "logical" pragmatism; the death of Vailati at the early age of 46 in 1909; the death of Calderoni at 35 in 1914; *Leonardo* ended in 1907; James died in 1908; Prezzolini converted to Crocian idealism; Amendola became a statesman and liberal; and Papini, in the latter part of his life, converted to Christian mysticism.[37]

The return of idealism in Italy, which was, in a sense, a reaction to the brief, but strong pragmatist movement in Italy, was due to two idealists, whose intellectual influence both fueled and supported the rise of fascism: Sergio Panunzio and Gentile. By 1914, Panunzio—who studied law at the University of Naples and moved through the schools of thought of positivism and scientism to philosophical pragmatism to critical idealism—was under the influence of a form of Kantianism, with its emphasis on individualism; through the works of Benedetto Croce, he had also been introduced to neo-Hegalianism and accepted many of its analyses. Because of these influences, Panunzio saw law as something that emerges from an inherently human process—not a fixed idea:

"Justice," Panunzio argued, "...like truth, was something that was in and with humankind," not something external. Justice, truth, and history were all products of "the incessant and irrepressible human spirit—divine because human."[38]

This informed Panunzio's proclamation after the end of the war that he expected Europe to start an era of systematic reconstruction after revolution, followed by an era of order and solidarity where humans "obey and serve, to be free within order and within a system, to not so much search for rights as they would for law."[39]

Panunzio, by the time the Fascist squads arose, believed in and was a part of articulating the doctrine of national syndicalism—one of the main components of the ideology of fascism—which was a fusion of nationalism and syndicalist organization:

> In November 1918, Mussolini himself identified national syndicalism as a doctrine that would unite economic classes behind a program of national growth and development. For the nation to emerge from the Great War as a potential member of the circle of victorious "great powers," it would be necessary to establish a "constructive" regime of "major production...a mode of reorganization of economic relations [calculated to generate] maximum return...National syndicalism will make of Italy...a greater nation."[40]

Panunzio's national syndicalism—in which he suggested that "natural law" was the basis of his conception of state, law, and society—was informed by Gentile, though it differed in some ways from Gentile's absolute idealism because Panunzio saw "natural law" as *transcendent to* human consciousness as opposed to *immanent in* human consciousness (à la Gentile).[41]

Gentile, meanwhile, conceived of a new state as a "political concept rooted in the antiindividualism of classical idealism," where his philosophy of Actualism,

> ...was eminently inclusive—one in which the empirical, solitary, "abstract," individual, together with classes of individuals, the leadership of the state, and the state itself, constituted, in Gentile's judgment, an integral moral unity—what Gentile chose to consider a collective, if pluriform, "concrete individuality."[42]

This idea of a collective "concrete individuality" was articulated by Gentile by 1918 when he spoke of the emergence of a "revolutionary state," where politics and morality, parochial and national interests, would come together in order for individuals to "fully identify themselves with [the state's] actions."[43] The combination of nationalism, Panunzio's national syndicalism, and Gentile's Actualism came together to provide the philosophical rationale behind the mobilization of the first Fascist "action squads." Soon after, when Mussolini became prime minister in 1922, he appointed Gentile to serve as his counselor.[44]

PIRANDELLO'S *SIX CHARACTERS IN SEARCH OF AN AUTHOR*

During the war years, according to famed Pirandello biographer Gaspare Giudice, Pirandello was heavily influenced by the "theatre of the grotesque" (whose playwrights included Alberto Casella, Luigi Chiarelli, Luigi Antonelli, Enrico Cavacchioli, and Massimo Bontempelli). Giudice quotes an article that Pirandello wrote in 1920 that suggests to Giudice that "[Pirandello] had moved closer to assimilating the grotesque almost in anticipation of *Six Characters in Search of an Author*." Pirandello wrote in this article:

> A fine definition of the most significant modern works of the grotesque is *transcendental farces*... Hegel explained that the subject, the only true reality, can smile at the vain appearances of the world. It stipulates it, but it can also destroy it; it does not have to take its own creations seriously ...[45]

My colleague and leading Schopenhauer scholar David E. Cartwright eloquently put it to me that the philosophies of the late nineteenth–early twentieth centuries—idealism, pragmatism, analytic philosophy, and phenomenology—were all "under the shadow of Hegel." Of course, this brief mention of Hegel cannot suggest that Pirandello was familiar with the Italian pragmatists and their reaction to British Idealism, or even intimately familiar with Hegel. But the fact that Pirandello used Hegel to explain the very theatre (i.e., the "theatre of the grotesque") that seemed to most influence the writing of his masterpiece, *Six Characters*, suggests that at least hints of the rational versus empirical debate may have made it indirectly into Pirandello's play, as Hegel was reappropriated by all sides of the rational versus empirical debate (and, hence, why Hegel was back in the limelight in intellectual circles). The greatest evidence that Pirandello was well familiar with the debate between idealism and pragmatism (or rationalism and empiricism, respectively) came from the public exchange of writings between Pirandello and Benedetto Croce. Croce was a very influential Italian idealist and the first exchange of writings between the two writers was in 1908 and 1909, then the very height of Italian pragmatism. Croce and Gentile's idealism, to a large degree, was one of the very reasons that Italian pragmatism only flourished for about the first decade of the twentieth century.[46] Giudice documents the initial exchange, which started in 1908 (and continued even after Pirandello's death) with the publication of two collections of essays by Pirandello, *Art and Science* and *Humour*:

> Pirandello opened the attack in *Art and Science* saying that Croce's *Aesthetics* was "abstract, incomplete and rudimentary," that it was "an intellectual aesthetic system without intellect," and that Croce "insulted logic" with false premises, sophisms, and contradictions, which resulted in "confusion." In *Humour* he dismissed Croce's opinions that humour was an indefinable psychological state, a pseudo-concept, and not an aesthetic category, and defended the aesthetic autonomy of humour.
>
> Croce replied almost immediately with a review of *Humour* which appeared in *La Critica* (VII, 1909). He showed that he was unaware of the attack in *Art and Science*, and he treated Pirandello condescendingly. He started off by asserting that Pirandello was unacquainted with the authors he cited in his essay... "But there is not much point in discussing it since Pirandello is far from strong in the field of methodology and scientific logic." Then he added: "I do not want to take advantage of his doctrinal inexperience... since the author's difficulties are quite evident ... "
>
> Despite his public declarations to the contrary Pirandello was convinced he was an expert in philosophy but, when confronted with Croce's self-confidence, he began to doubt his abilities... He then [11 years later, in 1920, when *Humour* was reprinted] changed a few pages and added a few notes in an attack on Croce. He accused him of bad faith. "It is not true that Croce does not understand. He does not want to understand"... "Croce's philosophy immediately becomes an iron gate which will not budge. We cannot get through! But what is behind the gate? Nothing. Merely this single equation:

intuition equals expression, and the affirmation that it is impossible to distinguish art from non-art, artistic intuition from common intuition."⁴⁷

These two dates, 1908–1909 and 1920, were very significant times for philosophy and Pirandello. In 1908–1909, as mentioned earlier, Croce was exerting his influence over the pragmatists through his idealism. In 1920, as also mentioned earlier, Pirandello had his mind on Hegel, which appeared to (directly or indirectly) influence his play *Six Characters* (and idealism was clearly in intellectual circles advocating for fascism). Thinking of himself as a philosopher, Pirandello clearly attacked some of the "logic" of idealism. Yet Croce saw this attack on "logic" as something coming from someone who "is far from strong in the field of methodology and scientific logic." It would appear that Pirandello was a pragmatist, and there is much in *Six Characters* to support that reading. However, that reading is not so clear-cut.

First of all, Pirandello supported Mussolini and fascism (though he did not commit himself fully to fascism until a bit after he wrote *Six Characters*). Seth Baumrin underscores the tension between Pirandello's support of fascism and his writings:

> It may seem ironic that Pirandello was on good terms with the ruling class. He publicly supported Mussolini, but his writing in no way reflects Fascist ideology; in fact, it may resist such authority.⁴⁸

While Giudice suggests that Pirandello was fascinated by the doctrine of action of the Fascists,⁴⁹ the idea of action aligns Pirandello with the Italian pragmatists (who, like Pirandello,) were at odds with the logic of Croce's idealism. However, the influence of Italian idealism on fascism by Panunzio and Gentile can also be seen in the disappearance of the individual to support state action. Thus, we have two equally valid readings of *Six Characters*. (1) Supporting pragmatism, reality is malleable (via Papini). It is action—the playing out of the characters' story—that transforms reality. The very nature of writing, then, is to construct characters (who represent our ideals, myths, and concepts) precisely to mold our reality. (2) Supporting idealism, the truths and ideals of the characters are there only to contrast the notion of a more abstract individual (as the characters are more concrete and real than the individuals in the play). The audience member, then, perceives the failures of individualism, but simultaneously realizes that he or she has discovered this truth in a collective environment (an audience). Given the validity of both readings, *Six Characters* becomes a tract, in a sense, debating the merits of idealism versus pragmatism.

Other Pirandello scholars have indirectly noted this tension between these philosophical schools of thought. Most notably, Roger W. Oliver discusses *Six Characters* in terms of the breakdown of human personality and objective truth: Pirandello exposes the multiplicity of personality, truth, and reality, erasing the idea that these ideas are monolithic and easily knowable.[50] Oliver suggests that this exposure of how reality and truth function is dramatized through the tension between the Father and the Director:

> [The Father] is arguing formally for the multiplicity of the personality and against the injustice of being known by only one facet of it... A man of reason has been caught in an act of passion and is now being threatened by constant identification with that act.[51]

Oliver continues:

> This failure [of the Director] to see is caused less by stupidity than by fear, a fear of the new. The Father presents a severe challenge to the notion that man is basically a rational creature who can maintain control over all aspects of himself, including his actions, his personality, and the way he is perceived by others. The Director is not ready to accept this challenge and the uncertainty it suggests, and he flees first into practicality and then out of the theater itself.[52]

Oliver frames the tension of *Six Characters* in terms of the multiplicity versus the absoluteness of truth. This line of thought postdates Pirandello's contemporary debates around Modernism (and simultaneously around pragmatism versus idealism). From Oliver, we can see hints of Pirandello challenging the notion of an absolute knowable reality through reason (via idealism), but we can also see how (via pragmatism) an empirical demonstration of truth also falls short (as the Father makes a strong rational case that he should not be defined merely by one of his own actions).

Anne Paolucci, leading Pirandello scholar, writes about *Six Characters* (and other Pirandello plays) in terms of Pirandello's Hegelian perspective of comedy and paradox. Paolucci limits her analysis of Pirandello's plays really to Hegel's notion of how comedy and tragedy work in Hegel's *Aesthetik*. In referencing Paolucci's essay, I am less concerned with how, Paolucci observes (via Hegel), "in comedy... the characters dissolve the world around them into laughter, yet rise above it all, their subjective personality persisting well-assured."[53] Instead, I am more concerned with Paolucci's passing argument put forth by Hegel (used to set up the essay about Pirandello's Hegelian type of comedy): "that the dissolution of art in the modern world coincides with that moment in history when individual freedom has been fully articulated."[54] I want to repeat a portion of what Pirandello wrote about the "theatre of the grotesque" in 1920, which Giudice suggests greatly influenced Pirandello's own *Six Characters*:

> Hegel explained that the subject, the only true reality, can smile at the vain appearances of the world. It stipulates it, but it can also destroy it; it does not have to take its own creations seriously...

When Pirandello's above quote is juxtaposed against the quote by Paolucci immediately above it about Hegel's view about the moment in history when "individual freedom has been fully articulated," we must draw out Hegel's insistence on the fact that a dialectic grounded in reason is the path to understanding absolute truth, via a type of Platonic idealism. Hegel's sense of individual freedom derives from the fact that, as Hegel contends, humans are the only things that possess a reality (understood through reason) that enables them to make moral and ethical choices. Note, then, that Pirandello does seem to misunderstand Hegel. According to Hegel, it is not that humans (or "subjects") are the "only true reality," it is, rather, that humans are the only ones who can *understand* a true reality because of their ability to reason (and, therefore, discover absolute truths).[55]

If we step back and assess Pirandello's view of philosophy, we get something of a mixed message. Pirandello was as an ardent attacker of Croce's idealism, which suggests that he might have favored something more in line of pragmatism (especially with a line like, "the subject, the only true reality," which appears to echo something closer to empiricism). On the other hand, Pirandello appears to like Hegel, who was a nineteenth-century German idealist, but also someone, with this small above evidence, Pirandello may have misunderstood. If we turn to the two above scholars, we delve even deeper, but no more clearly, into both Pirandello's idealism and pragmatism. Oliver's observation of the Father in *Six Characters*—that "The Father presents a severe challenge to the notion that man is basically a rational creature who can maintain control over all aspects of himself, including his actions, his personality, and the way he is perceived by others"—gives a nod to the action-based, anti-reason philosophy of pragmatism. And then we have Paolucci writing about Pirandello's Hegelian notion of comedy and paradox (which, indirectly, suggests that Pirandello was at least influenced by Hegelian idealism). My conclusion, then, is that Pirandello was not able, if he had indeed wanted to, to push a clear idealist or pragmatist agenda through *Six Characters*. However, Pirandello, who clearly fancied himself a philosopher, was using the philosophies (even if inexactly) that were being discussed in his era to explore the very nature of reality and how humans are able to understand that reality and the truths found there. Thus, I argue, *Six Characters* is an exploration of the debate between idealism and pragmatism.

The opening line of the play—"I can't see"—immediately presents the audience with the central problem surrounding *Six Characters in Search of an Author*. Just before the Manager tries to read a letter, the Prompter "*turn[ed] on a light.*" When the Manager calls for "a little light," then, the audience is confronted with an epistemological quandary: as there is a light already on at the rehearsal, why is the Manager calling for "a little light," since it would seem that there is *already* a little light on (i.e., in other words, why not ask for *more* light?)? Given that *seeing* and *light* are metaphors for knowledge as old as time immemorial, the Manager, like the audience, cannot truly see the rehearsal space: there are only two lights on (one at the Prompter's box and one, now, on the stage). The very nature of the play, and much of the reason it was innovative, comes from the fact that Pirandello is exposing the internal workings of the theatre. But the lighting gives the audience pause. Though the audience members see some of the stage and props, they immediately have to align themselves with the Manager when he first says he "can't see" and then asks for "a little light."

The Manager clearly frames the light, metaphorically framing the knowledge and the method with which it can be received.

Metaphorically, the audience cannot trust everything it sees (as the lights are only partially on). But the audience is also bound by what the Manager allows us to see, as he is the one who calls for the lights. This becomes a matter of the blind leading the blind. Therefore, if the audience cannot empirically understand the play (as the audience is not fully allowed to see everything and knowledge/light is mediated through the Manager), does the audience naturally turn to rationalism? Of course, if the audience continues its initial alignment with the Manager, then, by the end of the play, the audience will have learned nothing (as the Manager misses the truth and purpose of the "performance").

Where and when, then, does the audience break away from the epistemological influence of the Manager? When the Manager tries to explain Pirandello's play, *Mixing it Up*, the Manager's failure to understand the play alienates the audience:

> "The empty form of reason without the fullness of instinct which is blind." You stand for reason, your wife for instinct. It's a mixing up of the parts, according to which you who act your own part become the puppet of yourself.

The Manager's failure to understand the very thing he needs to understand (i.e., the play) in order to successfully define himself (as a director), is what alienates the audience, for it distrusts, now, the Manager's ability to frame a complex reality. The irony here is that the line—"you who act your own part become the puppet of yourself"—is referring to none other than the Manager. Because the Manager does not understand the play (one of the essential tasks for a director), the Manager is left acting as/performing to be a Manager/director. He "becomes the puppet of [him]self" because he still controls the strings of the performance, but he ventriloquizes his internal thoughts into a caricature of himself. There is a clear division between what the Manager says and his ability to do or understand what a director does or understands.

This becomes the ultimate confusion of the play: the Manager's inability to both see and understand the play(s) strips the Manager of the "essential" nature of a Manager/director. Yet, at the same time, every attempt he makes to "direct" the play of the six characters, he fails, and becomes a spectator for the six characters' play. Thus, as the play progresses, the Manager stops doing what a director does. And though he chooses to be a spectator (the audience), he fails at that too, for he is not transformed, for he cannot empirically or rationally see the dramatic event that unfolded before his eyes, furthering the notion that he is not/cannot be a director because he does not understand drama when he sees it.

The drama, then, I argue, is not with the six characters, but the inability of the Manager to take in truth. The six characters do represent the *absolute truth* of Idealism: these characters are essences, in part, because nothing they do can change them (for they are bound to what they do, as their existence is limited to what the author wrote about them). But the characters can also be thoroughly understood by pragmatism. For if they do not act out their drama—"live" as they say—they do not exist. But by acting it out, by living a drama—where if x works, then x is true—their tragic drama becomes true (and the enthralled spectatorship of the actors and the Manager suggests that there is the dramatic tension there). The Manager, though he has these two epistemological tools to understand what is in front of him, cannot understand the truth because he cannot understand that these are characters and is not, ultimately, convinced that their drama, which enthralled him, was dramatic or true.

The description of the characters, upon their arrival, is noteworthy. All of the characters, Pirandello writes, possess an "*essential reality of their forms and expressions.*"[56] This idea is most assuredly why Pirandello, in later versions of the play, had the characters wearing masks. The masks, in later versions, are physical manifestations of an internal, unchanging truth, specific to each character. If Pirandello does want to suggest that there is something so "essential" about each character, why, then, is the description of the Father so markedly different from those of the other characters? The details found in the description of the Father is absent in those of the other characters. Pirandello draws a portrait of a full, living, breathing "man":

> He who is known as the Father is a man of about 50: hair, reddish in colour, thin at the temples; he is not bald, however; thick

moustaches, falling over his still fresh mouth, which often opens in an empty and uncertain smile. He is fattish, pale; with an especially wide forehead. He has blue, oval-shaped eyes, very clear and piercing. Wears light trousers and a dark jacket. He is alternatively mellifluous and violent in his manner.[57]

In contrast to the other five characters, the Father is not a type of "everyman." Not that the other characters are without any specificity, but the details are of such a different nature. The Father and the rest of the characters appear to come from two different types of drama: the Father from a realistic play and the other characters from an expressionist play. In a sense, the conflict between the Father and the rest of the family is not only a conflict between reason and passion, but a conflict in how one is to present truth (i.e., realism versus expressionism).

Six Characters' tension, then, and probably the reason that audiences had so much trouble digesting the play, is the fact that Pirandello tries to present an expressionist play (with, arguably, the main character being a realistic character) in a hyper-realistic play. Thus, we get a mixed message when the Father describes the *truth* behind the characters:

> ...living beings more alive than those who breathe and wear clothes: being less real perhaps, but truer![58]

If there is something "truer" to the characters because of the fact that they are "fantastic characters"[59] who possess almost a "*dream lightness,*"[60] why, again, does Pirandello draw such a life-like portrait of the Father?

In contrast to the Father, there are no stage directions for what the actors or the Manager (or other people working at the theatre) look like or anything about their personalities. They are, after all, named only by their jobs, even less personal than Father, Mother, Son, et cetera. There are only a few names mentioned in this play and each deserves a bit of attention. First, in the opening of the play, while the actors are rehearsing *Mixing it Up,* the Manager, in order to direct the actors, refers to the characters of *Mixing it Up*: "When the curtain rises, Leo Gala, dressed in cook's cap...Guido Venanzi is seated and listening."[61] The Manager here has an opportunity to call the actors by their real names, but chooses instead to refer to them by the names of their characters. This can suggest that the actors, in the eyes of the Manager, have become indistinguishable from their characters. Immediately after, the audience finds out that *Mixing it Up* is a play by Pirandello.[62] This is a reference to a real 1919 play by Pirandello (in Italian it is *Il giuoco delle parti*, commonly translated as *The Rules of the Game*). The inclusion of a real play and Pirandello's name helps ground this play in the real theatrical world of post-1919 Italy. Pirandello, it should be noted, is the only "real" name of a "real" *person* in the entire play. Maybe this is a suggestion by Pirandello that *theatre* is a very real and true enterprise. A little later, when trying to explain how characters live for an eternity, the Father mentions the names of two "real" characters, "Sancho Panza" and "Don Abbondio."[63] The mention of these names forms something concrete for the audience, which is lost, along with the Manager and the actors, with the audience and the characters (i.e., the Manager and the actors) trying to wrap their heads around the idea that a character *can* exist and live forever. Soon after, the Step-Daughter tells of Madame Pace, the head of the brothel that the Father visited and where the Step-Daughter worked. And finally, when the Manager is trying to stage a scene of the characters, the Manager says that the Mother needs a name:

> THE MANAGER: . . . (To the Second Lady Lead:) You play the Mother. (To the Father:) We must find her a name.
> THE FATHER: Amalia, sir.
> THE MANAGER: But that is the real name of your wife. We don't want to call her by her real name.
> THE FATHER: Why ever not, if it is her name?

Why do both Madame Pace and the Mother, Amalia, get named? If this is indeed the drama of the Mother as the characters say it is, then to humanize the story, we need to know who made all of this possible (i.e., Madame Pace) and the name of the central character of the family drama (i.e., the Mother/Amalia).

Another reason that the Father is drawn as life-like, I argue, is that the Father is the only "director" that we see in this play, and, as such, is the only "human" or individual present in *Six Characters*. In traditional Western theatre (except in Brechtian and collaborative theatre), of all of the humans associated with the *production* of a play, the director is the only "real" individual who should be presented. (One could make a good argument that we should be able to see the playwright as well, as the play portrays a view of reality from the playwright's eyes. However, the playwright, almost all of the time, is not involved in the *production* of the play. And *Six Characters* is about producing a play.) In other words, the audience sees what the director wants us to see; we see the play through the mind of the director. While the actors are front and center in a performance, we only see a residual part of their individuality: their job is to make the character come alive (and implicitly, how the director sees that character coming alive). That is not to say that the actor is just a puppet, for there are significant acting choices to be made all of the time. But in successful acting, the audience should not be thinking about the skill of the actor (something that can come after the production). A successful actor makes the audience forget the fact that he or she is acting.

The director, on the other hand, especially in adaptations of canonical plays, should be able to present a familiar plot as something new and different (though still capturing the essence of the play). The choices that the director makes (as opposed to the actors), then, should come through: the director develops the epistemological frame (i.e., the director decides how the truths present in the play should be presented and understood). But especially in productions that are not just playing the play "straight," the director makes the audience aware of the play's epistemological frame. In other words, truth is presented through the frame of the director.

Why, then, do I call the Father the "director" of the play? The Manager, as I already suggested, is not essentially or experientially a director. And certainly, the Manager does not understand that he creates the epistemological frame of a play:

> LEADING MAN (to the Manager): Excuse me, but must I absolutely wear a cook's cap?
> THE MANAGER (annoyed): I imagine so. It says so there anyway (*pointing to the "book"*).

The Manager finds himself subservient to the text and not an active participant in creating a telling of the text. The Manager does not understand, even more so than States' observation that the actor *is* the story that he or she is telling, that a director *re-creates* the (playwright's) story that the actors are telling.

The Father, on the other hand, lives the same story/plot as the other characters. But the Father, more so than any of the other characters, tries to frame their story in terms of his version of the truth and the truth about himself. The Father, thus, attempts to be the director of their drama, to create an epistemological frame for his audience (an audience composed of the actors, the Manager, and us). The Father's story, how he frames the characters' reality, is a story of trauma, of a man and a family in crisis: a story that would ring true, or ring too true, to post-WWI Italians.

If the Father is the only "human" in the play, then why does *he* not have a name? The answer might lie in the fact that maybe post-WWI Italians could see themselves in the Father: not necessarily as an "everyman," but as a post-WWI Italian.[64] The compounding crises that arise over the course of years for the family of characters force the Father to confront himself. The Father is (for 1921 Italians) the new face of psychoanalysis. He psychoanalyzes himself in a rational manner (using one part of himself), while trying to make sense of the hard-to-admit horror of his, as I mentioned earlier, "uncontrollable and invisible psychological urges" (that constitute the other part of himself). The trauma of meeting his Step-Daughter in her roles as a prostitute (realizing it only as the Mother screams and rushes in after he makes his sexual intentions clear) is the thing that forces him to reconcile these two parts of his self:

> *THE STEP-DAUGHTER*: But imagine moral sanity from him, if you please—the client of certain ateliers like that of Madame Pace!
> *THE FATHER*: Fool! That is the proof that I am a man! This seeming contradiction, gentlemen, is the strongest proof that I stand here a live man before you. Why, it is just for this very incongruity in my nature that I have had to suffer what I have.[65]

The "contradiction" in the Father is not just the contradiction of morality/immorality, but also the contradictions of reason/the irrationality of passion, character/man, and "*alternatively mellifluous and violent in his manner.*" The Father is almost a Hegelian dialectic all in himself. The truth that emerges about the Father for the audience is presented to us through his contradictions. Post-WWI Italy must have presented itself as a contradictory place: the Great War was over, but the crises continued. Post-WWI

Italians must have been able to relate to the "crisis at home." As can be seen from the historical portrait of post-WWI Italy earlier, the "home" that the soldiers returned to, looked awfully different. The family's crisis, started by the Father sending away the Mother and ending at Madame Pace's brothel, spawned a crisis in their home, creating instability that literally and metaphorically resulted in death.

The intellectual climate of the day, again, was that of change, especially with the destabilizing ideas of Einstein and the Dadists. The challenges to logic, which we see presented in the Father's own speeches, must have echoed the challenges that the Italian pragmatists presented: Panini arguing that reality is malleable and Prezzolini's attacks on logic. Here is where I fully agree with Oliver's assertion that the Manager is scared of the new and the uncertainty that the Father presents. But while these attacks from the Father could very well be a veiled attack by Pirandello on Croce's logic and the need people have for logic, the destabilizing nature of the *Six Characters* for the Manager—and although the Manager does not change, he is many times an audience member as well—causes the Manager, not to retreat to logic, but to ignore what happened the entire day. It is almost as if Pirandello suggests that in Italy's return to idealism (via Gentile and Panunzio)—which was influenced heavily by his arch-nemesis, Croce—Italians retreated from the new, unsettling views of nature. But then again, Pirandello was himself a lot like the Father, a Hegelian contradiction: like the Father, a clear advocate for humanity, but—in Pirandello's own support of fascism—as blind to it as the Manager.

Conclusion

Anthony Petruzzi reads *Six Characters in Search of an Author* through Heiddeger's idea of discourse. The truth that Petruzzi is discussing is that of the characters.

> The *personaggi* cannot control the dissemination of their positionality, of their words, of their "essential" nature; the *personaggi* cannot control their own self-presentation.[66]

It is important to note, though, that the audience changes (especially in 1921 Italy during its premiere run), but nobody on stage changes. The audience is aware that the characters cannot change. However, when the actors and the Manager assume the role of the audience, especially the Manager's inability to be changed by the drama complicates the conceptual framework of the Actor-Audience Relationship (discussed in the introduction). The conceptual framework that Petruzzi set up, then, can be applied even better to the Manager (and the actors) to elicit a new understanding of the play (especially considering its historical and philosophical moment).

The actors, who are used to *being* the story they are telling (via States' idea that "the actor is... a kind of storyteller whose speciality is that he *is* the story he is telling"[67]), cannot accept that fact that the characters *are* the story. This is an affront to the actors, as the actors subconsciously realize that there is a primacy in their own roles that can never be reached, for the actors are telling the story, one layer removed from being the story. For the actors, this is, how Petruzzi suggests, the Heideggarian "primal conflict": the annunciation of the incarnate thought into a public becomes embodied thought. Once the embodied thought is spoken by the actors to an audience, the incarnate thought withdraws from the actors (as their speech is not in the realm of public interpretation).[68] The six characters, without an author and (and more importantly) an audience, *are* simply incarnate thought. The characters are the speech; they are the story; their story cannot be open for interpretation and is fixed (in an "essentialist" manner) without an audience.

Here, though, I disagree with Petruzzi, because the embodied thought of the characters does change with each different audience (for the audience, as well, contributes to the context of the play), while the incarnate thought of the characters never does, and never will, change. While Petruzzi says that Heidegger suggests that being is a process and that "Pirandello's style is a phenomenological description of the process of the disclosure of the truth," the problem lies in the fact that being is not a process for these characters. When the actors try to act out the characters' story, the characters laugh (and rightly so). The characters even get upset because the characters realize what Heidegger suggests:

> ...every occurrence of articulate self-understanding frames an object with prejudgements that concomitantly conceal the object

under consideration. The process of revealing can never be separated from what is also concealed, or covered-up, by our insufficient understanding.

For the characters, they cannot frame their story this way or that way: they are their story. The actors, however, are the ones who frame the truth of the characters, and every choice that each actor makes both reveals a truth, but also frames it in such a way that the revelation of truth can never be attained. Thus, each time the actors tried to play the characters' story, their portrayal was just as true as it was false. *And this is the burden of the theatre: stated in an almost-utilitarian philosophical manner, the director must maximize the revelation of truth while minimizing what is concealed through the play's telling.*

CHAPTER 3

1952 PARIS: *WAITING FOR GODOT* AND THE GREAT QUARREL

> En attendant, essayons de converser sans nous exalter, puisque nous sommes incapables de nous taire.[1]
>
> In the meantime let us try and converse calmly, since we are incapable of keeping silent.[2]
>
> —Estragon in *Waiting for Godot*

1952 PARIS WAS NOT A SILENT PLACE. Earlier, after the bombs fell on Europe, there was not exactly calm after the storm. Even though a renewed hope in peace briefly followed the end of the war, immediately after there was the overwhelming prospect of rebuilding Europe after the devastation it had endured.[3] As I attempt to show, the nonlinear historical *progression* following WWII provided 1952 Paris with a situation rife with philosophical conflict. The philosophical (and, in a sense, political) debate that Camus and Sartre had in *Les Temps modernes* in mid-1952 was indicative of the historical moment, much like the philosophical conversations that Samuel Beckett engaged with in *Waiting for Godot*. I argue that *Waiting for Godot* explores the same (epistemological) dilemma that Merleau-Ponty says defined his era: being versus doing.

POST-WWII FRANCE

As Tony Judt argues, three problems were in the forefront in the first 18 months following the Allied victory: a lack of food, a devastated German economy, and the lack of American dollars.[4] Judt sums up the sense of hopelessness that most Europeans felt in 1947 by quoting Janet Flanner, who was reporting form Paris in March 1947:

> There has been a climate of indubitable and growing malaise in Paris, and perhaps all over Europe, as if the French people, or all European people, expected something to happen, or worse, expected nothing to happen.[5]

Europe and Europeans certainly felt a sense of despair: the sense of despair so often read in plays from the "absurdists," if you will, like Beckett's *Waiting for Godot*.

However, on June 5, 1947, US Secretary of State George C. Marshall announced what was later to be called the Marshall Plan, which was to change not only the economies of Europe, but fundamentally changed the attitudes of Europeans. The Marshall Plan's psychological benefit to Europeans was palpable:

> *The Times* was not so very wide of the mark when it stated, in a leader on January 3rd 1949, that "(w)hen the cooperative efforts of the last year are contrasted with the intense economic nationalism of the inter-war years, it is surely permissible to suggest that the Marshall Plan is initiating a new and hopeful era in European history."
>
> The real benefits were psychological. Indeed, on might almost say that the Marshall Plan helped Europeans feel better about themselves. It helped them break decisively with a legacy of chauvinism, depression and authoritarian solutions. It made co-ordinated economic policy-making seem normal rather than unusual. It made the beggar-your-neighbour trade and monetary practices of the thirties seem first imprudent, then unnecessary and finally absurd.[6]

The path to feeling better began with an economic plan, which included aid through annual requests.[7] The United States also poured in dollars to furnish a credit pool that came to be the Bank of International Settlements. This "Bank" offered lines of credit to each country proportional to its trading requirements, "contribut[ing] not merely to the steady expansion of intra-European trade but to an unprecedented degree of mutually advantageous collaboration."[8] This liberalized trade created a postwar economic boom stemming from, not the prewar emphasis on "protection and retrenchment," but "sustained commitment to long-term public and private investment in infrastructure and machinery."[9]

But the changes following WWII were not just economic in nature. The political landscape of the world was changing. With the Korean War and the Cold War, especially building up between the United States and the Soviet Union, always in the background, new colonial and postcolonial concerns arose.[10] For years, French schoolchildren saw "France" as extending well beyond its natural borders, where the "cultural attributes of Frenchness were open to all."[11] After the liberation in 1945, France's colonial reach was vast. But the loss of Indo-China was a "political and military catastrophe."[12] North Africa later became the center of France's attention. However, the attention was not always there: the French government simply quashed an Arab uprising in the Kabylia region east of Algiers in May 1945, demonstrating that France was indifferent to Arab sentiment.[13] It took the November 1, 1954, Algerian insurrection and the formation of the Algerian FLN *(Front de Libération Nationale)*, followed by eight years of civil war, to get France to focus on North Africa.

While 1952 Paris did not have the kind of political upheaval that was soon to preoccupy the French with the civil war in Algeria, in 1952, France, and particularly Paris, was also undergoing a cultural upheaval. Part of this cultural upheaval had to do with the increase of an automobile culture. With the introduction in 1947 of the first French car to be mass produced and affordable, the "people's car," the Renault 4CV, production could not keep up with demand as there were thousands times more buyers than cars. Culturally, as Ross suggests, automobiles offered people a new mobility that allowed them to break with the past and gave them a new attitude toward mobility and displacement.[14] But this cultural upheaval also had to do with the "generalized postwar atmosphere of moral purification, national cleansing, and literary laundering."[15] In a sense, Ross suggests, the new focus on actual hygiene in France derived its power from that fact that France and its women needed to be clean so that it could maintain its metaphorically clean role in it colonies. But with the continual loss of the colonies, the French must turn inward to the home, "as the basis of the nation's welfare."[16]

Though Milward suggests that the economic boom was a phenomenon of the 1950s that started in 1950 and wound down in the 1960s, that is not to say that Europe, and France, was economically in the clear.[17] Maybe the result of these lingering economic struggles or the result of cultural shifts, the leading topic of the day in postwar France, then, centered around the pro-communism/anti-communism divide and the use of political violence.[18] Many youth were attracted to the "leadership, direction, discipline and the promise of action in harness with 'the worker'" that characterized the PCF (French Communist Party).[19] But the realities of the crimes committed in the name of communism were not easily ignored by all.[20] Among the intelligentsia, the debates in public raged mostly through those *categorized* as "existentialists." Maurice Merleau-Ponty suggested that the new dilemma was "being versus doing" and that one must engage in History.[21] In this respect, the French claimed to have learned about the inevitability of political violence.[22] "The Great Quarrel," as it is sometimes called, sprung from these debates. The entire above history—political, economic, and cultural—found itself squeezed into a contentious debate that simmered over in Paris over the course of 1952 between Albert Camus and Jean-Paul Sartre.

"The Great Quarrel"[23]

A short literary, philosophical, and political history of Sartre and Camus is still needed to situate the Great Quarrel in the milieu of 1952 Paris.[24] Sartre was *the* French intellectual in postwar France.[25] David Drake, in *Intellectuals and Politics in Post-War France*, notes that *Being and Nothingness* (1943) established Sartre as a philosopher; *The Flies* (1943) as a playwright; the first two volumes of *Roads to Freedom* (1945) confirmed him as an author; writing with the underground press as a literary critic and then later as a journalist; thus, following the war, there was no one in France who paralleled Sartre's literary reputation.[26] Thus, with the cofounding and subsequent success of *Les Temps modernes* (first published in October 1945), Sartre was at the center of the postwar intellectual world.[27] And Sartre's prominence was highlighted by what Beauvoir later called the "existentialist offensive": in addition to *Les Temps modernes,* 1945 saw the publication of two existential novels—Beauvoir's *The Blood of Others* and Sartre's *The Age of Reason*.[28]

Maybe because of this fame, intellectuals, following the waning of *épuration* after the Liberation passed and German capitulation, positioned themselves in relation to existentialism and/or the Marxism of the PCF.[29] The PCF, until Sartre's rapprochement with the PCF in 1952, viewed Sartre with a great deal of suspicion. Sartre, in the PCF's eyes, "was a degenerate *petit bourgeois* writer, the epitome of idealism and individualism [which contrasted with hierarchical discipline of democratic centralism and the cult of the leader of the PCF] who rejected the materialistic 'scientific' truths of Marxism, and who was a friend of the 'traitor' Paul Nizan to boot."[30] Sartre's individualism, in the mind of the PCF, contrasted with the ideals of Marxist theory in that, as Marxist historian Auguste Cornu writes, the Sartrean individual is "an absolute subject with his *raison d'être* in himself."[31]

While Sartre was upset and wanted the support of the PCF, Camus, on the other hand, feared a PCF takeover and supported Malraux in 1946, who saw the Soviet Union as the principal danger to world peace. Writing in *Combat* in November 1946, Camus delivered a harsh critic of Stalinism.[32] Though there was a period up to 1951 when these two friends shared some ideas (both participated in the *Rassemblement Démocratique Révolutionnaire* [RDR] and the two became closer during the rehearsal of Sartre's play *The Devil and the Good Lord*, which opened in June 1951), the publication of Camus' *The Rebel (L'Homme révolté)* in October 1951 opened up a furious debate that divided the two from there-on-out.[33] This was on top of the always-building tension between Camus and Sartre due to their different social and cultural backgrounds (Camus came from working-class roots in Algeria, while Sartre came from a "literary Parisian *petit bourgeois* household").[34]

In hopes of sidestepping the need to define Camus' philosophy of the absurd and rebellion and Sartre's existentialism (as the purpose of this book is not to explore these philosophies, per se),[35] I hope that examining the differences, rather, between Camus and Sartre will sufficiently give the reader an overall sense of both philosophies. The opening pages of Camus' *The Rebel* offer a strong rebuttal to nihilistic existentialism, of which Sartre is the principal philosopher. Camus' *The Myth of Sisyphus* (1942) argues that in order to make life have meaning, humans must confront the absurd: a situation where one's desires are contradicted by the realities of the world. Suicide, Camus argues, cannot be a legitimate answer, for suicide makes revolting against and contemplating the absurd impossible.[36] In *The Rebel,* Camus continues his idea of revolt with the idea of rebellion, where, "with rebellion, awareness is born."[37] As opposed to existentialist nihilism, where, "if [Camus'] age admits, with equanimity, that murder has its justifications, it is because of this indifference to life," Camus' essentialist view that humans are good leads to the idea that "from the moment that life is recognized as good, it becomes good for all men."[38] Camus' sense of humans as essentially good derives from Camus' sense of the existence of human nature. Royle describes the difference, what he calls "perhaps more fundamental than any," between Camus and Sartre's sense of the existence of human nature:

> Camus continues to believe in the existence of human nature, Sartre denies that there is any such thing: for him there is neither human nature in general nor anything natural in individual human beings. This is, of course, in part what he means by him dictum that for man existence precedes essence: nobody is born a coward—a person makes himself a coward through his actions, which he always remains free to change.[39]

For Sartre, since God does not exist, humans are the only thing whose existence comes before its essence. As Sartre bluntly states in "Existentialism is a Humanism," "Man is nothing else but that which he makes of himself."[40] On the other hand, in recognizing that "Man is the only creature who refuses to be what he is," Camus' rebellion, unlike that of the nihilistic existentialists, does not justify universal murder, but rebellion "can discover the principle of reasonable culpability."[41] In fact, rebellion finds its justification in human solidarity in that suffering (which in absurdism is an individual suffering) is a collective experience in rebellion, for one must realize that he or she, in suffering, suffers like the rest of humanity: from the distance that separates human reality from the universe.[42] Camus, like the existentialists, may argue that life has no inherent meaning, but unlike the existentialists, life is not made meaningful through experience/actions that affirm and define existence (the central tenet of the existentialists where *existence precedes essence*), but through the use of human reason (where reason justifies the statement, *essence precedes experience*). Camus literally plays off of the rationalist *par excellence,* Descartes, in forming the creed of rebellion and ethical revolt: "I rebel—therefore we exist."[43] In other words, my suffering proves that we are all human, for we all suffer. In short, Camus is primarily concerned with the meaning of existence, as opposed to Sartre, who focuses on the philosophical sense of being and the existentiality of existence.[44]

I used mostly *The Rebel* to bring these two philosophers into greater relief because it was, in fact, the publication of Camus' *The Rebel (L'homme révolté)* in October 1951 that set off the public intellectual debate in mid-1952. The key texts of this public debate, which appeared in *Les Temps modernes,* were (1) the review of Camus' *The Rebel* by Sartre's colleague Francis Jeanson, in the May 1952 issue of *Les Temps modernes,* and (2) Camus' rebuttal in the August 1952 issue, which also contained responses by Sartre and Jeanson. As Ronald Aronson, in *Camus and Sartre: The Story of a Friendship and the Quarrel that Ended It,* put it: "For fifty years The Rebel has demanded of those who read it to take sides. And for good reason. Between the middle of October 1951 and the summer of 1952, Sartre and Camus dramatically took positions concerning the Cold War."[45] These philosophers and their philosophies were not immune to the realities of post-WWII French (and European and world) history.

Jeanson's initial review takes aim at Camus' metaphysical rebellion, which, Jeanson claims, is abstract in the fact that Camus ignores history and how real history affected real people. Camus' metaphysical rebellion, in a sense, is so metaphysical that it turns Camus into a "passive atheist" who never denies God and sets the rebel up in opposition to God in "a pure metaphysical conflict in which there is no role for men and their history":

> The rebel ... is the victim who presents a permanent challenge and who does not give God the satisfaction of contemplating failure—because he plans nothing and therefore cannot fail.[46]

Because Camus, Jeanson argues, has relegated rebellion to the intellect without the context of real historical event, Camus has created an illusion by projecting a pure rebellion only based upon itself.[47]

Camus' response was equally as harsh and personal in its impersonal tone, as he referred over and over again to Jeanson, not by name, but as a "your collaborator." Camus accuses the "collaborator" of having, more or less, criticized him through a very selective reading that ignores much of what Camus actually wrote: "against all evidence, [Jeanson turned my book into] an antihistorical manual and the catechism of abstentionists":

> He has, in fact, adamantly refused to discuss the central theses to be found in this work: the definition of a limit revealed by the very movement of rebellion; the criticism of post-Hegelian nihilism and Marxist prophecy; the analysis of the dialectical contradictions concerning the end of history; the criticism of the notion of objective guilt; etc. On the other hand, he has discussed in detail a thesis that is not to be found there.[48]

Camus largely examined the flaws of Jeanson's argument, saying that Jeanson was criticizing what was not there and ignored what was there.

If the tone of Jeanson's review and Camus' response was harsh, Sartre's tone and subject matter were violently personal. In essence, Sartre accuses Camus of taking it personally due to, as Sartre argues, Camus' "struggle within [his] own heart."[49] Sartre continues on this personal psychological attack:

> Your personality, which was real and vital as long as it was nourished by events, became a mirage. In 1944, it was the future. In 1952, it is the past, and what seems to you the most intolerable injustice is that all this is inflicted upon you from the outside, and without your having changed.[50]

Though Sartre echoes Jeanson's idea that Camus rejects history, he does so in the utmost of personal ways by calling Camus, himself, "an abstraction of a rebel": "You became violent and a terrorist when History, which you rejected, rejected you in turn."[51] Sartre's closing line prophetically sealed their relationship: "But whatever you may say or do in return, I refuse to fight you. I hope that our silence will cause this polemic to be forgotten." After this article was published, the two never spoke again.[52]

In a large sense, the public exchange of letters was nothing more than the airing out of dirty laundry between friends due to building tension from their more and more divergent philosophies. In this sense, from a philosopher's standpoint, these letters did little to shed new light on their respective philosophies. However, the soap opera that unfolded in print in mid-1952 Paris, fascinated the public by showing the two philosophers and their philosophies at such odds that they would sever a friendship. However much or little the letters revealed about their philosophies, the fact was that this battle thrust the two thinkers (and their battle) into the national limelight. Aronson puts the importance of these articles in context. *Les Temps modernes,* a Paris journal, had a circulation of just over 10,000. When the August 1952 issue came out, it immediately sold out, reprinted, and sold out, again. Outside of *Les Temps modernes,* the exchange of letters was republished in *Combat,* the paper Camus once edited; discussed in over a dozen newspaper and magazine articles with sensational headlines; as Sartre's friend, Raymond Aron said, these articles, "immediately assumed the character of a national dispute."[53] This national dispute between Camus and Sartre, I argue, was played out in the pages of Beckett's *Waiting for Godot* (which itself turned into a sensation).

BECKETT'S *WAITING FOR GODOT*

Admittedly, Samuel Beckett did not write *Waiting for Godot* in Paris in 1952.[54] It is well known that he had been shopping around for a theatre to produce the play since he wrote it between 1948 and 1949 in French *(En attendant Godot).* It can then be argued that *Godot* was not a product of 1952 Paris, but of an earlier Paris where food was more of a concern than making art. However, there is also a plausible explanation as to why *Godot* did not first appear to the public until October 1952 (it was published then in Paris by Les Éditions de Minuit, and was not produced until January 1953). Maybe, it can be suggested, Paris was not ready for this play. Though it is hazardous to even suggest that *Godot* is *about* this or that, it clearly appears to be philosophical in nature. In a sense, in 1948 and 1949, who even had time to contemplate finer points of philosophy? How does a nation embrace an avant-garde conversation when that very same nation is simply trying to put food on the table? The question on people's minds was, how do we rebuild Europe? True, art is edifying. But art cannot be appreciated, or more importantly, have any affect, when one's stomach is growling. Needs that stem from survival supersede the pursuit of anything else: even when that anything else is pleasurable or important for the cultivation of the human mind and culture. As is demonstrated by the above history, the concerns of the nation, especially around 1948–1949, were about food, safety, money, reimagining Europe, and securing basic goods.

But as the economy improved, the needs and desires of the populace changed accordingly. As Milward points out, before 1950 people used their disposable income for basic necessities: food, clothing, and furniture.[55] However, when one contrasts that to the fact that after 1949 consumer consumption turned to new innovations—such as radios, vacuum cleaners, sewing machines and, especially, cars[56]—one can easily make the connection that survival was no longer on people's minds, but instead, people (1) had disposable income for nonnecessities and (2) used that disposable income for, what were at the time, luxury goods. In the sense that survival is a necessity, art is a luxury.

Thus, by October of 1952, Paris not only was in a much more financially stable place where people could start turning their minds to the finer things in life, but anyone who followed the newspaper was also thoroughly aware of the debate that raged between Sartre and Camus throughout 1952. Newspapers in France in 1952 no longer had to constantly report death tolls, treaties, political realignments, and troubling news about the economy: as soon as life could go on without fear of financial, cultural, and political collapse, the question of *meaning* could be taken up again. Thus, France not only had an opening for Sartre and Camus to debate, but it must have been so long since people could not only take in what they were saying, but looked forward to the luxury of forgetting their troubles and focusing, instead, on themselves (as both Sartre and Camus' philosophies largely debate the question of "me," in a sense, and "my" place in the world). Thus, late 1952 Paris was now ready for a play like *Godot*.

Furthermore, just as Esslin's *The Theatre of the Absurd* made it very apparent that theatre goers needed a new framework in which to see and understand the ahead-of-its-time and, frankly, difficult play, *Waiting for Godot*, it is also equally possible that the debate between Sartre and Camus helped shape the reception of the play as existential. (And it must be remembered that Camus was seen as an existentialist at the time.) Since existentialism was in the air and debated and understood as a concept, existentialism (especially as explained through the more intellectually approachable exchange of letters among Camus, Sartre, and Jeanson) possibly provided a framework in which to understand *Godot*.

Though the differences between Sartre's existentialism and Camus' "existentialism," at the time, was not seen as Camus' *split from* existentialism, as I said earlier, Merleau-Ponty said that the central debate of the time was one of "being versus doing." This, to a large degree, is the debate that I argue Beckett is having within *Godot*. As Vladimir says—modifying Hamlet's famous question about being—"What are we doing here, *that* is the question." The last image we have of Estragon and Vladimir is a confusing one, but drives home the point of Merleau-Ponty's articulation: Estragon says, "Yes, let's go," but the following stage directions read, "*They do not move*." Though I do believe that Beckett, ultimately, suggests a Camusian reading of the world as is demonstrated by my chapter on *Godot* in my book, *Reassessing the Theatre of the Absurd*,[57] I argue that the central dilemma *debated* in *Godot*, hinted at by the quagmire that Beckett presents in the last instant of the play, is, do we need to *do* to affirm our existence, or do we need to *be* to make life meaningful?

I want to briefly discuss three relatively recent productions of *Waiting for Godot* that demonstrate the tension of *being versus doing* that, I argue, is inherent in the play. A production of *Waiting for Godot* in St. Petersburg by director Yuri Butusov in 2001 presented a traditional, "absurd" reading of the play. The audience was greeted by a hangman's noose: eliciting from the reviewer the response of, "Death, flight, and nothingness?"[58] Because the focus was on absurdity and nothingness, the despair of this production emerged because there was nothing or little *to do* to be able to affirm one's existence (producing a Sartrean reading of the play).

I was fortunate enough to see (and review) Anthony Page's production of *Waiting for Godot* on Broadway in 2009. Page, on the other hand, did not appear to read the play as an, "existential cry from the abyss nor a meditation on despair."[59] Instead, presented basically as a comedy, this production's most energetically delivered line was, "And I resume."[60] I believe that this line, being the focal point of the play, reveals an emphasis on *being*. Given that Lucky seemed to come to life when he repeatedly said the line, "I resume," I read this line, not as focusing on the *action* of *resuming*, but as focusing on the *resumption* of the *I*.

Paul Chan's *Godot* contained *both* Camus' concept of *being* and Sartre's concept of *doing*. Situated in Hurricane Katrina-devastated New Orleans, Chan staged the play in two locations: one in the Lower Ninth Ward and one in Gentilly. The house in Gentilly simply existed to give meaning: "The very fact that the house had survived, standing, registered as a triumph."[61] In a sense, the house only had to *be* in order to make the play meaningful: demonstrated by the very fact that the house stood in defiance of the absurdity of Katrina (both the natural disaster and the response [or lack thereof]). On the other hand, the most important line, or "the soul of *Godot*," as suggested by the reviewer was, "... Let's do something, while we have the chance! ..."[62] The reviewer's concluding line, referring to Chan, was, "An artist—an unusual one, to be sure, and rarely idle—saw a chance and made the most of it." Especially, in the Gentilly performance, the emphasis on both being and doing could be simultaneously seen and understood.

* * *

The famous opening stage directions read: "*A country road. A tree. Evening.*" In a sense, we are confronted with the same type of predicament as when we look at Goya's "The Dog" (1820–1823). The painting of a dog's head peaking out over a vast stretch of sand under a huge sky, recalls a paradox of the human condition: the dog is in a liminal state when confronted with an absurd situation, as the dog is simultaneously swallowed by the reality of the world, but is capable of looking upwards.[63] In other words, as Victor Frankl contemplates, how is it that some people in the face of suffering can find the will to go on? Thus, we can see the solitary tree, without leaves, as a symbol of life in the face of the absence of life. This set becomes meaningful through the combination of space and gesture (yes, gesture). Two simultaneous readings are generated, each one representing one side of the Sartre-Camus philosophical schism: (1) the tree is a defiant affront to a world empty of meaning by the very nature that as essentially a tree, despite its seemingly distraught state, it affirms the existence of life, or (2) though the tree appears to be lifeless, the fact that it is a tree and cycles through metaphorical life and lifelessness foreshadows the fact that it will do what trees do and grow leaves once again (as it does at the beginning of Act II), both metaphorically coming to life and *becoming* a tree by *doing what trees do.*

Determining which reading is more appropriate for an audience member depends upon which part of the set they focus on: the tree, the vast emptiness, or most importantly how the viewer sees the tree's relationship to the emptiness. Three readings spring up from the last observation. (1) If the viewer notices more of the emptiness of the stage, then the viewer may understand the set in terms of Sartre's concept of *nothingness,* which is more or less the absence of being. (2) If the viewer notices the tree more than the emptiness, then the viewer may understand the set in terms of Heidegger's concept of *nothingness,* from which *being* springs (and Heidegger explicitly said he was not an existentialist). And (3) the viewer may take an entirely different approach based on either visual situation and understand the set in terms of Camus' concept of defiance, where the tree continues to live in defiance of the lack of life surrounding it. How the viewer reads this scene also depends upon whether the audience member understands nonaction as a sign of lack of action or as a sign of choosing inaction. (A tree of course does not decide anything, as I am personifying, but the tree is an obvious metaphor for how humans, in this case Vladimir and Estragon, respond to the world.)

The set is important for another reason—this time directly concerning the arguments made in the exchange of articles in *Les Temps modernes* between Camus and Sartre (and Jeason): is the set more or less empty because it is a play about a metaphysical rebellion and does not need to be couched in history but, rather, in the mind, or is the set a very real (though metaphorical, of course) response to the penury due to the devastation of WWII? It is a problematic question because the answer also depends upon how the characters are played: as mouthpieces of metaphysical philosophy who, in effect, do nothing throughout the play; or as active participants in life, who despite the injustices of the world (as represented by the master-slave relationship of Pozzo and Lucky),[64] are able to actively rebel and make their lives meaningful.

The first few lines of dialogue that open up the play echo this empiricist-rationalist debate in the use of juxtaposing words and gesture. In the first line Estragon says, "Nothing to be done." First, it is an ironic statement as Estragon is sitting there *doing* something that needs to be done (i.e., the removal of pain): Estragon is trying to remove his boot as he believes something in the boot is giving his foot discomfort. The audience member must, then, choose whether to believe his words or his actions, for they seem to contradict one another.[65] If we focus on the removal of the boot, then do we concentrate on his doing something, or do we concentrate on the fact that he continues to struggle despite the fact that the task appears so hard that he has to keep giving up?

Estragon's words, though on the surface, suggest a Sartrean reading of the world. "Nothing to be done" suggests that if we cannot *do* anything, then in a sense, we cannot exist, as our being is a result of our doing. However, if we break down the construction of this phrase, we notice its peculiar phrasing: the verb *do* is conjugated as a passive verb, "to be done," therefore containing both the idea of "to be" and "to do." This conflation of Sartrean and Camusian elements of existence continues immediately after in Vladimir's response:

> I'm beginning to come round to that opinion. All my life, I've tried to put it from me, saying, Vladimir, be reasonable, you haven't tried everything. And I resumed the struggle.

Vladimir simultaneously accepts a metaphorical nothingness and rejects it. His "opinion," what he believes, is that there is "nothing to be done," but in using reason he rationalizes that that statement cannot be true unless he has "tried everything." Vladimir is aware of the fallacy of the statement, "nothing to be done." At the same time, however, though his actions confirm he "resumed the struggle," the fact that he "tried to put it from [him]" through reason suggests that reason is not a perfect science, that maybe it is fallacious, as well.

Almost coming out of the struggle that he has been "*musing*" on, Vladimir turns to Estragon and *sees* him:

> *VLADIMIR*: So there you are again.
> *ESTRAGON*: Am I?
> *VLADIMIR*: I'm glad to see you back. I thought you were gone for ever.

Playing off the return of the Prodigal Son, Vladimir, who thought Estragon was gone, is happy to see his return. But the fact that Estragon is unsure of his return is a telling statement. Is the "am I?" a response to the idea that he exists (highlight the "you are") or is Estragon puzzled because he feels that he never left. Estragon sleeps in a presumably nearby ditch (as Estragon's "over there" implies that the ditch is more or less within seeing distance) and it is Vladimir who appears to leave every night (since (1) Vladimir entered at the beginning of the scene while Estragon was already there, and (2) if Vladimir was also nearby, he would have known/seen Estragon at night, given that Estragon was nearby). Why is it Vladimir, then, who is surprised, in a sense, to see that Estragon is back when Estragon never really left? Why is it not Estragon saying the same thing to Vladimir (where the lines are reversed)?

The response of "Am I?" is potentially the central question of this play. This is one of the most significant translations into English that Beckett makes, for the French text reads "Tu crois?" or translated more literally as "you believe?" or "you think?" First, the subject of the question changes from "you" to "I." Then the predicate changes from "believe/think" to "be." Therefore, the entire idea of the question changes. In a sense, the idea of *you believe* must be asked as a question for someone else's belief cannot be truly known by the speaker of the question, whereas am I/I am can only be known, in a sense, by the speaker who is the only person who is privy to his or her own reasoning and is the only one who has been present for every action that he or she has done. Therefore, "you believe?" implies a degree of uncertainty because it has to be uncertain, whereas, "Am I?" implies a degree of uncertainty where there should, rather, be certainty.

Once in the English (as translated by Beckett), the key to Estragon's question is the phrasing of it. Beckett does not write the question as "I am?" thereby repeating the precedent of the structure that Vladimir sets up, "...you are...," which implies a question of I am *what*? This phrasing (i.e., "I am?") would suggest a question of what am I doing on this earth, but less of a sense of a much more basic question, do and how do I exist?[66] "Am I?" suggests a much deeper philosophical question regarding the existence of the self. The emphasis with "Am I?" is on the verb "to be." The question then becomes a question of, is the act of *being* actually *me*? Am *I* defined by my *being*? Or is my *being* define by *me*?

This question is addressed just before Pozzo and Lucky make their first appearance in the play, Vladimir and Estragon have a brief conversation about character:[67]

> VLADIMIR: Question of temperament.
> ESTRAGON: Of character.
> VLADIMIR: Nothing you can do about it.
> ESTRAGON: No use struggling.
> VLADIMIR: One is what one is.
> ESTRAGON: No use wriggling.
> VLADIMIR: The essential doesn't change.
> ESTRAGON: Nothing to be done.

It is very important that Beckett chose the words "temperament" and "character" to begin this mini-conversation. The definition of "temperament" as it was first applied to humans (as opposed to compounds, natural things, etc.), stemmed from the medieval sense of humours: "In medieval physiology: The combination of the four cardinal humours of the body, by the relative proportion of which the physical and mental constitution were held to be determined."[68] In a sense, humans, then, were born with their own unique combination of the four cardinal humours and their, corresponding, physical and mental constitution did not change. "Temperament" is closely connected and defined in part as "disposition," which is the "natural tendency or bent of the mind."[69] Likewise, with the first definition of "character" as used in the everyday sense of the word, we see the idea of something innate, natural, and essential: "The aggregate of the distinctive features of any thing; essential peculiarity; nature, style; sort, kind, description."[70]

Vladimir and Estragon's reaction to this essentialist view of human nature only confirms what the two words imply: "Nothing you can do about it"; "No use struggling"; "No use wriggling"; and "Nothing to be done." In short, no matter what you "do," your essence will remain the same: your *actions* will not change your essence. As Vladimir states very succinctly, "The essential doesn't change." The line, "One is what one is," could simply be seen as an extension and/or reiteration of "The essential doesn't change." However, given that this line is playing off of the Old Testament line from God, "I am what I am," this line deserves its own attention.

The very fact that the line is changed to no longer imply God, rests this statement solely in the human realm. But this statement is, more or less, stated as a proof, much like Descartes "I think, therefore I am." Not only does the line, "One is what one is," provide an essentialist understanding of the world and of human nature, but it is stated as a logical maxim or even, to be creative, like the final part of a syllogism. The maxim or the conclusion of a syllogism can only be arrived at, not through experience, but through logic and reason.

Almost immediately after Pozzo and Lucky's exit, we see a very different conversation. Before Pozzo and Lucky come in, the two tramps have a grasp of an essentialist view of human nature. In the larger sense of essence preceding existence in relation to *Waiting for Godot,* the characters are not defined by their actions. This has to do, in part, with each characters' temperament and disposition. But more importantly, their essences' are reinforced by their own use of reason. Pozzo, for example, is a master, not just because of how he treats Lucky, but because of how he rationalizes his relationship with Lucky: "He wants to impress me, so that I'll keep him"; "He wants to mollify me, so that I'll give up the idea of parting with him."

Though reason makes the world a meaningful place for Pozzo, it is also a horrifying way to justify the use of violence and oppression. In a sense, this simplistic essentialist view falls apart in the face of Pozzo's reasoning (who can easily be seen as a metaphorical "collaborator"). Thus, we have the polemical battle over the use of political violence (hashed out between Camus and Sartre) hovering in the background. We can see both viewpoints. Camus' reason has its limits; Sartre's justification of murder is just as oppressive as Pozzo's treatment of Lucky. It becomes impossible to ignore the faults of Pozzo and, thus, after they leave, Vladimir (more of the philosopher of the two) needs to imagine a world where there exists a possibility that people can change. That idea becomes necessary for Vladimir to make sense of the world. However, this idea also has its limits. As Camus points out:

> Man is the only creature who refuses to be what he is. The problem is to know whether this refusal can only lead to the destruction of himself and others, whether all rebellion must end in the

justification of universal murder, or whether, on the contrary, without laying claim to an innocence that is impossible, it can discover the principle of reasonable culpability.[71]

What Camus warns against is that people can change for the worse. And thus, when Vladimir suggests to Estragon that Pozzo and Lucky have changed, we are left guessing as to did they change for the better or worse:

> VLADIMIR: How they've changed!
> ESTRAGON: Who?
> VLADIMIR: Those two.
> ESTRAGON: That's the idea, let's make a little conversation.
> VLADIMIR: Haven't they?
> ESTRAGON: What?
> VLADIMIR: Changed.
> ESTRAGON: Very likely. They all change. Only we can't.
> VLADIMIR: Likely! It's certain. Didn't you see them?
> ESTRAGON: I suppose I did. But I don't know them.
> VLADIMIR: Yes you do know them.
> ESTRAGON: No I don't know them.
> VLADIMIR: We know them, I tell you. You forget everything.
>   (Pause. To himself.) Unless they're not the same...

The question becomes, what type of change did Pozzo and Lucky undergo? In a sense, both philosophies have a problematic tension with the idea of change. In simplistic Camusian rationalism, the essentialist reading suggests that despite what is *done* by the two, in a sense, Pozzo and Lucky's essence remains (essentially) the same. Whereas, in simplistic Sartrean existentialism, the empiricist reading suggests that despite everything else that Pozzo may do in his life, he is an oppressive slave owner by his actions,[72] and thus though his actions could or may have changed, his previous actions cannot be undone and thus he is defined forever as a slave owner (think of Sartre's *No Exit* where a character who murdered is a murderer).[73]

Vladimir is fascinated by the supposed change in Pozzo and Lucky, while Estragon (1) does not consciously notice it, for he would not have to ask "who?" and (2) and tries all he might to change the subject by not addressing the aspect of change in Pozzo and Lucky, but turning it into a generalization. It begins to make sense that Estragon wants to change the subject because the subject of change hits home too hard: "They all change. Only we can't." But Vladimir will not leave this topic alone. Could it be that Vladimir, the philosopher of the two, does not see what it obvious to the corporeal Estragon: that the two cannot change?[74] This is a possible reading, for though Vladimir may provide the philosophy, Estragon is "[his] only hope." This even suggests that philosophy (of Sartre or Camus) does not hold up to the observations of everyday life.[75]

Estragon's notion that he does not know Pozzo and Lucky while Vladimir insists that they do know them brings up the question of who judges *being*. Does Vladimir *know* them through Pozzo and Lucky's actions, and their actions alone? Can Vladimir even know them this way? Or does Vladimir know enough about their inner life to feel as though he knows them? Does Estragon, in another sense, thinks that he knows Vladimir?

The idea of how change is viewed by Beckett (or the audience, for that matter) depends upon who is looking and from what vantage point. Act II opens up, notably, with the tree now having "four or five leaves." The question of change and being, thus, continues in the second act:

> *VLADIMIR*: ...I was saying that things have changed here since yesterday.
> *ESTRAGON*: Everything oozes.
> *VLADIMIR*: Look at the tree.
> *ESTRAGON*: It's never the same pus from one second to the next.

The idea of change is problematic in looking at the tree. A Camusian reading would suggest that, in a sense, nothing has essentially changed: the tree is still essentially a tree, despite the fact that it has leaves on it. A Sartrean reading could come to the same conclusion in that, in growing leaves, a tree is doing what a tree does.

Beckett suggests that being is not an either/or (Camus/Sartre). The key word here the intransitive verb, *ooze*: "to pass slowly or in small quantities through the pores of a body or through small openings or interstices; to exude, to seep."[76] The sense of ooze is that is passes through the boundaries of an object. In a sense the object does not contain that which it oozes. Therefore, what is being oozed comes from within but is on its way out of the object. In a sense, what oozes is liminal, neither of the body of the object nor of something distinctly not of the body. By Estragon calling the tree a "pus," he metonymically defines the tree by the very thing that oozes from within the tree to out of the tree. In a sense, *being* can no longer be defined by a sense of self, but the self's context in now drawn into the picture. The oozing nature of the tree, or "everything" for that matter, makes *"being" a misrecognition of the self,* as we could imagine Jacques Lacan (who influenced many 1960s and 1970s French intellectuals) saying if he were a psychologist who studied *being* from the point of view of a philosopher. While Beckett engages with Camus and Sartre, he moves beyond the two thinkers, suggesting that in oozing, we have the ability to constantly go beyond our boundaries, beyond the physicality of the body, beyond the confines of the mind. In a sense, we are part being, part meaning, and most importantly, part of the world.

Conclusion: Mr. Godot

Beckett famously said in response to Alan Schneider's question about who is Godot, "If I knew [who Godot was], I would have said so in the play." Therefore, the important thing is not who is Godot or whether he really exists, but *how* does Godot exist in this play and for what purpose?[77] Though Camus and Sartre's philosophies vary wildly in many respects, in a sense, the principal preoccupation of the two philosophers is the idea of existence. For Sartre, we exist because we act, and our actions leave traces that we exist. For Camus, our existence has meaning because we have reasoned it so. Godot's existence depends upon both how his actions affect the world and how we create the meaning of Godot in our heads.

However, although Godot can be understood in terms of Camus and Sartre's differing philosophies[78]—Godot exists through the messages delivered by the boy (Sartre) or Godot exists because he gives us meaning and, thus, Godot exists within us (Camus)—Beckett's sense of oozing, I think, provides the best sense of Mr. Godot. In a sense, Beckett engages with the present debate between existentialists (namely Sartre) and rationalists (namely Camus) to anticipate a future conversation lead by Jacques Lacan.[79]

In oozing, Godot exists in a liminal manner: he is body, he something distinctly not his body, and he is that which passes in between. In a sense, then, Godot is everything and nothing, and everything in between that. Godot is the ultimate phenomenologically relative idea. Godot is also the ultimate rationally relative idea. Godot, in his penultimate incarnation, is, in fact, whatever the audience member needs him to be to make sense of Beckett's *Waiting for Godot*.

CHAPTER 4

COLD WAR TACTICS: FEAR IN *WHO'S AFRAID OF VIRGINIA WOOLF?*

> GEORGE: Who's afraid of Virginia Woolf
> Virginia Woolf
> Virginia Woolf,
> MARTHA: I... am... George...
> GEORGE: Who's afraid of Virginia Woolf...
> MARTHA: I... am... George... I... am...¹

THE COLD WAR. The confrontation of global superpowers. Nuclear armament. The United States versus the Soviet Union. Democracy versus communism. Good versus evil. The United States was a scary place in 1962. The world had a lot to be *afraid* of.

Edward Albee's work has, at times (in academic literature), been grouped with the Theatre of the Absurd because of Albee's similar "radical devaluation of language."² In a particularly relevant essay, Jeane Luere observes terror and violence found in Vienna's English Theatre's 1987 production of Albee's *Who's Afraid of Virginia Woolf?* Luere argues that this terror and violence is an adjunct of the same "omnipresent issues of communication, awareness, and identity" found in "the works of his peers Beckett, Genet, and Pinter."³ Though this reading is suggestive, Luere's reading relies on the all too common readings of miscommunication.⁴ However, though I believe that the cause of terror and violence found in these plays is more complex than these communication breakdowns, I do generally agree with Luere's conjecture of the importance of terror in Albee's play. The play is, after all, called *Who's AFRAID of Virginia Woolf?* (MY EMPHASIS). Though not discussing terror in any respect, Jill R. Deans was onto something when, writing about Albee's *Box*, she argues, "there and not there, both defined and empty, the 'box' resembles adoptive subjectivity, present in absence."[5] I would like to play off of Deans' assertion and suggest that in *Who's Afraid of Virginia Woolf?* George and Martha's "son" is a conceptual "box" that serves as a holding place for the "present in absence" in order to ease their feelings, not exactly of terror, but more specifically, of *fear* (and I will return to the difference later).[6] This reading is significant because, as Deans observes that *Box* is "one of Edward Albee's most existential dramas,"[7] my reading places Albee's *Virginia Woolf?* outside of the sole province of existentialism.

The fear in this play does not derive from existential angst. Though the idea of the "present in absence" connotes a form of affirmation of existence, the preoccupation of the characters is less about whether they exist and how their existence defines them, but more about the question, how are we to live *and* be happy? In a sense, *Virginia Woolf?* is a carefully crafted psychological drama that engages the issues of existential existence while simultaneously suggesting the use of reason can be used to triumph over fallacious defense mechanisms.

However, though deriving his philosophical understanding from and participating in the same "being versus doing" (and the engagement in History) debate[8] that Beckett tussles with in *Waiting for Godot*, Albee moves beyond that debate and dwells, instead, on the debates within philosophy that were more contemporary to both his time and place: the simultaneous birth and death (or rebirth) of analytic philosophy. As a conceptual "box," where George and Martha's "son" represents the "present in absence," the philosophical debate is over logical positivism's principle of verification and analytic philosophy's response, where the "son" "exists" as a rational concept, but observation is impossible. George and Martha's Wittgensteinian "language-games" describe their everyday life, their reality. Here, I am engaging with *Virginia Woolf?*'s history of being read through the "games" that George and Martha play.[9] However, thinking about their "games" both literally and metaphorically as "language-games" (via Wittgenstein), this reading allows us to see through the "son" as a *conceptual box* that stands for the "present in absence" that masks the *real* situation: the *fear* of facing the *real* world, without a conceptual comfort blanket that imposes false purpose and meaning upon George and Martha's existence. These "language-games" destroy the conceptual box of the "son," but provide George and Martha—and the audience—with a truer *description* of their and our reality. Though like other absurdists, Albee clearly plays with language, in a major departure from conventional Albee scholarship, these "language-games," then, with their focus on language and how it is really *used*, suggest not that Albee *devalues language* (as is supposedly characteristic of absurdist playwrights), but rather, the exact opposite: Albee places an *increased value on language* and its ability to, ultimately, describe reality.

Stephen J. Bottoms notes that J. L. Austin's seminal study of analytic philosophy, *How to Do Things with Words,* was posthumously published the same year as *Virginia Woolf?*[10] Bottoms briefly suggests that *Virginia Woolf?* enacts some of the emphasis on performatives discussed in Austin's work.[11] Continuing off of Bottoms' suggestive remarks, I argue that in the end, the "son," as well as the philosophical legacy of logical positivism, is killed off by a J. L. Austin speech act: George's "performative" statement, "our...son...is...DEAD!"[12] But this "performative" also "kills off" the philosophical skepticism that knowledge is never knowable. True, their son in never *knowable,* but the events in George and Martha's life, their "history," is both factual and experiential and that the science of logical positivism (represented by Nick) cannot take into account history's "glorious variety and unpredictability."[13] It is "the surprise, the multiplexity, the sea-changing rhythm of...history" that gives life its humanistic quality, and love—George and Martha's love—its un-easily identifiable, but complex richness.

The Cold War and Civil Rights: The United States in 1962

Much in the same way that we have seen that "new" philosophy is a *response to* an "older" philosophy, so too might we say that the JFK-led 1960–1962 period (as I am limiting these years to the appearance of *Virginia Woolf?*) was a reaction to the Eisenhower-led late 1950s. The seeds of the 1960s may have been sown in the cultural rumblings of the late 1950s. Classically, the late 1950s were seen as a period of "blandness" and "optimism" as public opinion polls at the time seemed to suggest; however, James T. Patterson and some other scholars cite evidence of "cultural unease": the "Beats"; early rock n' roll (Chuck Berry and Elvis); the comedians Lenny Bruce and Tom Lehrer; the widely discussed 1957 essay by Norman Mailer called "The White Negro," celebrating a "hip," loose lifestyle; and various political dissenters.[14] This view is furthered by the fact that opponents of the conservative status quo (especially after the recession in 1958) began making headway in politics, with Democrats capturing many seats in the 1958 election and the emergence of John F. Kennedy.[15] But it was not only at home where Americans started to sense unease. The landing of *Sputnik* in 1957 caused Americans to react "with an alarm approaching a panic."[16]

Once Kennedy became president, there were three forces that constrained Kennedy's foreign policy and hardened the Cold War: the continuing power of the military-industrial complex; anti-Communist public opinion; and Khrushchev's provocative behavior.[17] There was also the very real aspect of fear when Kennedy began his presidency:

> The wide-spread fear of Communism fueled by the ugly excess of McCarthyism had not yet run its course, leading many Americans to believe that a Communist monolith headquartered in the Kremlin had devised a blueprint for world conquest that threatened the Free World and forces the United States to take the lead in a war on all fronts.[18]

Of course, all of this came to the forefront with the Bay of Pigs invasion on April 17, 1961.[19] Despite being a horrific failure, Kennedy continued his support of Special Forces and secret CIA-led efforts to undermine governments abroad.[20] Kennedy's continued obsession with Fidel Castro and the Bay of Pigs affected Kennedy and Khrushchev, as a *"mano a mano* emotionality imparted ... Soviet-American relations in 1962."[21] The result was a "missile crisis," as the Soviet Union began sending, first, military personnel in 1961 and, then, missiles in 1962 to Cuba.[22] After Kennedy publicly and privately warned Khrushchev to not arm Cuba and Khrushchev denied doing any such thing, on October 15, 1962, U-2 reconnaissance flights took photographs of Cuban missile sites, which led Kennedy (a week later) to say that any missile shot at places in the Western Hemisphere would provoke a "fully retaliatory response" upon the Soviet Union: "unprecedented fear and tension gripped people throughout the world in the immediate aftermath of this announcement."[23] "What kept war from breaking out," John Lewis Gaddis surmises about the fall of 1962, "was the irrationality, on both sides, of sheer terror."[24]

However, even with the intensification of the Cold War, Kennedy's presidency was celebrated.[25] Of course, though a beginning-to-boom economy may have been a huge factor in Kennedy's popularity, even more so than the 1950s—where upwardly mobile Americans were able to rejoice at the thriving economy that brought material comforts along with it—the 1960s was the longest period of uninterrupted economic growth in US history.[26] Industries such as electronics, which fueled the boom in the 1950s, continued even more growth in the 1960s, while businesses and professionals became used to a world of high-speed air travel, credit cards, and expense accounts, all in a world being transformed by explosively growing suburbs and the designing and construction of high-rise buildings.[27]

The Baby Boomers, as they came to be known, were growing up in a United States where they were personally unaffected by the Depression or WWII; their numbers breeding more self-conscious and more self-confident individuals.[28] Many now attending colleges and universities, "their brimming 'can-do' certitude stimulated grand expectations about the capacity of government to solve social problems," changing attitudes about what were perceived as entitlements (which were privileges just a generation earlier) and about "winning 'wars' against contemporary problems, ranging from poverty to cancer to unrest in Vietnam."[29]

The changing world and attitudes around them were reflected (or furthered) by a number of provocative and influential books that questioned conventional notions about American society and culture: Jane Jacobs' *Death and Life of Great American Cities* (1961), Joseph Heller's *Catch-22* (1961), Rachel Carson's *Silent Spring* (1962), and Michael Harrington's *The Other America* (1962).[30]

These anti-Establishment books reflected also the emergence of groups of protestors. 1962 saw the SDS radicals' Port Huron Statement—the manifesto of New Left activism; James Meredith's attempt to attend the University of Mississippi as its first black student (and subsequent retaliatory violence by segregationists which forced Kennedy to send in the army); and the formation of the National Farm Workers Association organized by César Chávez and other migrant workers.[31] Of course, needless to say, much of the late 1950s and early-to-mid-1960s had to do with Civil Rights, most particularly for African Americans.[32]

The United States in 1962 was at a crossroads. It was the height of fear of nuclear war, but was on the precipice of easing tensions. The economy was picking up steam, but it was just before the major decade-long boom. The Civil Rights movement was in its infancy, but just starting to coalesce. And with it, future social upheavals were beginning to take form with books and art and comedians, et cetera, who were beginning to challenge the status quo. And undoubtedly, *Virginia Woolf?* sat on this very same precipice, which, in a sense, took theatre goers on a tour de force that left them unable to ever go back.

THE BIRTH AND DEATH (OR REBIRTH) OF ANALYTIC PHILOSOPHY

The "birth" (if, like any movement or school of thought, is traceable at all) of analytic philosophy goes all of the way back to the Oxford Hegelians/Oxford Idealists that we encountered in Chapter 1. The figure at the height of the British Idealist movement, F. H. Bradley, was also the principal target of the attack that brought down idealism (or at least made it go out of style). Stewart Candlish's book, *The Russell/Bradley Dispute: And Its Significance for Twentieth-Century Philosophy*, documents a long debate between the prominent idealist Bradley and the first-emergent-then-prominent challenger to idealism Bertrand Russell. Russell, though not truly a "logical positivist" himself (a "logical atomist," rather), certainly influenced Ludwig Wittgenstein who, in turn, influenced the Vienna Circle, from whence logical positivism fully emerged. The analytic philosophy that we see in the latter half of the twentieth century developed out of the reaction to the logical positivists.[33]

In short, reacting to the vagueness of argumentation of the idealists, first Russell and then the logical positivists tried to turn philosophy into a science whereby the scientific method and scientific language were used to fuse rationalism and empiricism. Following Gottlob Frege,[34] Alfred North Whitehead and Bertrand Russell's *Principia Mathematica* (vol 1–3, 1910–1913) first aim was to show that mathematics was a branch of logic; their second aim was to show that mathematical logic is an ideal language that best captures ordinary language.[35]

Wittgenstein's 1921 work, *Tractatus Logico-Philosophicus,* paved the way for logical positivism by way of The Vienna Circle,[36] and A. J. Ayer's *Language, Truth and Logic* (1936) was arguably the penultimate study of this philosophical movement.[37] Interestingly enough, the most profound challenge to logical positivism came from one of its own: Wittgenstein. The later Wittgenstein wrote *Philosophical Investigations* (written over the course of much of the 1940s, but posthumously published in 1953), whose thesis was that logical positivism was not able to take into account the complexity of language; thereby, Wittgenstein studies the *use* of language. In addition to Wittgenstein's *Philosophical Investigations,* two other seminal texts laid the groundwork for analytic philosophy: W. V. Quine's essay "Two Dogmas of Empiricism" (1951) and Wilfrid Sellars' *Empiricism and the Philosophy of Mind* (1956). Quine attacks the logical positivists for their rationalist form of foundationalism. Sellars, on the other hand, argues that everything "is a linguistic affair," whereby he sees knowledge as a social practice, thus attacking the logical positivists for their empiricist form of foundationalism. Possibly the "end" or "death" of logical positivism came about in 1962 with the posthumously published collection of essays by J. L. Austin (who died in 1960), entitled *How to Do Things with Words.* It was Austin's concept of "performatives" that provided the final nail for logical positivism's coffin. (Austin's idea of "performatives" also paved the way for performance studies, which occupies the pages of this book's conclusion.)

Logical positivism had three central tenets: a sharp distinction between analytic and synthetic statements, the principle of verification, and a reductive thesis concerning the role of observation in order to determine cognitive significance.[38] Arguing that all propositions must be either analytic or synthetic (and never both), the logical positivists suggested that analytic propositions (tautological, *a prioi* propositions such as "All wives are married," which is true because by a definition a wife is a married female) give no information about the world; while synthetic propositions (factual, empirical, *a posteriori* propositions such as "All wives are mortal" where mortality is not part of the definition of wives and therefore past experience/observation are the only way to establish this truth) can give information about reality (when its assertions correspond to facts).[39] The principle of verification asserts that a proposition must be empirically verifiable (through observation or past experience) if it is to be meaningful.[40] In short, a proposition is nonsensical if we cannot understand it through observation or past experiences. The reductive thesis argues that all factual knowledge can be reduced to observable data.[41]

Logical positivism died out because of three main objections: an internal debate over the principle of verification and how does one go about verifying; the difficulty in precisely defining the principle of verification; and J. L. Austin's speech act theory's "performatives," which appear to be statements, but by not making an assertion or a claim, are neither true nor false (thus, the principle of verification would suggest that these performatives, such as "I now pronounce you man and wife," are nonsensical, meaningless statements, but, of course, everyone knows what statements like this mean.[42]

In *Philosophical Investigations,* Wittgenstein turns away from what he sees as traditional philosophy, which he sees as a *conceptual* activity based on non scientific ways to understand the world dominated by theorizing and explanation. In Wittgenstein's new conception of philosophy, he argues that the task of philosophy should be *description* (as opposed to *explanation*), giving the reader a true picture of things through describing resemblances and differences (in different scenarios or "cases"):[43]

> According to Wittgenstein, a traditional philosopher is "captured by a picture." This "picture," or "conceptual model," allows one in the grip of it to see deeply into things, making connections that the ordinary person would miss... Wittgenstein's alternative to this mode of philosophizing emerges from his new method. According to that method, philosophy is not a fact-finding discipline, but its function is to change one's orientation to and understanding

of reality. It does this by calling attention to facts one has known all along but that are so obvious as to be ignored or dismissed as unimportant.[44]

Trying to bring philosophy back to how language is used, Wittgenstein, for example, examines a metaphysical musing on *time* in Augustine's *Confessions*.[45] Whereas Augustine complicates the notion of time by trying to create a conceptual picture of what time is, Wittgenstein argues that anyone who uses the vocabulary associated with time "correctly" (i.e., following the rules of native speakers), already has a mastery of the *concept* of time.[46] Wittgenstein also uses "cases" and "language-games" to make his point that, as Stroll says, "philosophy is not a fact-finding discipline, but its function is to change one's orientation to and understanding of reality."[47] "Cases" for Wittgenstein are descriptions of something from ordinary life in a particular context; these "cases" should be compared and contrasted to provide an accurate view of reality.[48] "Language-games" are used to show how the same words have many different meanings which deconstructs Augustine's (and Russell's) idea that there is a specific idea behind every word (or as the earlier Wittgenstein writes in *Tractatus*, "The name means the object. The object is its meaning").[49]

Appearing in 1962 in a posthumously published collection entitled *How to Do Things with Words*, J. L. Austin's speech act theory was fully explained. After defining a number of utterances and types of "acts" and "forces,"[50] Austin argues that the "traditional view" of language is to see whether or not an utterance is true or false (based upon "propositions," "statements," and "assertions").[51] Austin introduces the idea of "performatives" to show the limitations of the "traditional view." The act of uttering "I do" at a marriage ceremony for the bride and groom is an example of a "performative." A "performative" (or "I do," in this above context) looks like a statement, which can be grammatically classified as such, but while there is nothing "true" or "false" about a "performative," it is meaningful and fully comprehensible, thereby challenging the notion of the logical positivists that an utterance much be either true or false to be cognitively meaningful.[52]

The tensions and preoccupations of the philosophy of the late 1950s and early 1960s can best be summed up in *Virginia Woolf?*, as a matter of fact. While it is highly unlikely that Albee had the same intimate knowledge of analytic philosophy that, say, Wilde had with Hegelian Idealism or Pirandello had with Italian Idealism, *Virginia Woolf?* thematically deals with the very questions that preoccupied thinkers like Wittgenstein and Austin: (1) George's discipline, history, is all about observation and past experiences, while Nick's discipline, biology, reeks of the scientism of the logical positivist; (2) George, especially, plays types of "language-games" in order to, as I quoted Stroll earlier, "change one's orientation to and understanding of reality"; and (3) George utters "performatives." 1962 saw analytic philosophy emerge as the dominant philosophy due to the "performative" metaphorical killing of logical positivism with the appearance of the concept of "performatives." Analytic philosophy was concerned with language as it is, and not what language as it could be.

Albee's *Who's Afraid of Virginia Woolf?*

It can easily be argued that George and Nick are adversaries (fighting for Martha's attention, in a sense, spurred on by Albee creating an obvious distinction between history and biology); Martha and Honey are secretly adversaries (fighting for Nick's attention); George and Martha are adversaries (fighting over an absent child); and Nick and Honey are secretly adversaries (for the same reason as George and Martha). I think a very persuasive reading, given the topic of fear and the historical context, could be that George and Martha can be seen as the two superpowers who pull the rest of the world of the play into the orbit of their tactical "games" for superiority, all the while forming and changing alliances for positional advantage for their next move.[53] While this reading is suggestive, it is reductive and becomes an allegorical treatise on the state of Albee's contemporary world of politics.

While "terror" certainly existed in the United States in 1962, except for the brief moment when George fires the (toy) gun, *Virginia Woolf?* is not a play that captures the "sheer terror" of (the threat of) nuclear war. Instead, as Patterson suggests about this time period in US history, this play is about "unease." Like watching an episode of television's *Curb Your Enthusiasm* with Larry David, the audience finds him or herself uneasy when sitting through this play.

It is uncomfortable. Nobody in the audience wants to be a part of a private, intimate fight by a couple of strangers.[54] The audience, just like Nick and Honey, walk into something usually done behind closed doors. And that is why this play is a perfect example of "Realistic theater," for the *fourth wall* is exposed for us to face "man's condition as it is"; showing our ugly side, in the presence of strangers, nonetheless, is uneasy for us to encounter.[55]

And these feelings of the audience's "unease" are captured much better in, especially, Martha's sense of *fear,* not terror. "Terror"—"The state of being terrified or greatly frightened"[56]—has much more of a connotation of the fact that what one is afraid of is actually present, while "fear"—"The emotion of pain or uneasiness caused by the sense of impending danger, or by the prospect of some possible evil"[57]—has much more of a connotation of the worry of a future arrival of something that will cause terror. *What is going to happen?* is the question that causes both fear and unease. With the United States and the world, in fact, at such a crossroads in 1962, there is something so unpredictable about the immediate future. What is going to happen next? And what will the world look like tomorrow? The nature of being at a crossroad meant that it was unclear as to which way the country would turn next. With the escalation of the threat of nuclear war, the beginning of an economic boom, the infancy of the Civil Rights movement, and the seeds of future social upheavals taking root, *what is going to happen?* was on the mind of many Americans, metaphorically embodied by America's "first family," George and Martha (i.e., Washington, D.C.), who shepherded the country through a *great American experiment,* through an uncertain era in American history.

And this is why George's sense of history so embodies the play. While one usually assumes history is the study of the facts of the past (and hindsight provides certainty of those past events), history, by George's estimation, also examines the uncertainties of the future[58]: "history...will lose its glorious variety and unpredictability. I, and with me the... the surprise, the multiplexity, the sea-changing rhythm of... history..."[59] This is also why we see the influence of analytic philosophy in the play. Analytic philosophy responded to the scientism of logical positivism. Language is a living and breathing organism that analytic philosophers realized could not be pinned down to a science, but its *use* could be understood in much of the same terms that George describes history.

While the toy gun captures the brief "terror" in the play and explores some of the issues at play in *Virginia Woolf?* about performatives, the doorbell raises some of the central questions of the play about "fear" and how it functions in the play. First, since Albee's text never indicates that the audience sees George ring the doorbell, we can presume that neither the doorbell nor George's action of ringing it is part of the visible set. It is also not really an off-stage sound, either, though, as the doorbell is both exterior and interior to the house. And second, the doorbell functions as a "performative," with the chime being neither a true nor false statement, but, in effect, its sounding, as the messenger of the "bad" news, literally and metaphorically delivers the same pronouncement and effect on reality as "our...son...is...DEAD!" But this raises the all-important question, can an inanimate object "utter" a "performative"? Of course, the doorbell has no intentions, but the effect of ringing the doorbell, though making an extra-lingual sound, is a part of our human vocabulary.

The sound of a doorbell, for someone inside, means, "there is someone at the door," while for the person sounding the bell, it means, "I am at the door." Of course, from the inside, it is unknown who is on the outside. Until the door is opened, there is a moment of that feeling, "who will I see when I open that door?" In the middle of the night, there must also be a feeling of fear, as private world of the house presumably shuts out the external, public. And the alarm and surprise of an invading external public creates an uneasy feeling once the doors are locked and the lights are turned low or off.

However, in this case, the delivery of the bad news, the confirmation that one's fears were justified, was not by someone external to the house, but by someone inside (i.e., George). This suggests two things: (1) what we have to fear does not come from an outside source (e.g., not the Soviets and Communists), but from ourselves, and (2) we are also the only ones who can *deliver* ourselves from our own bondage. George, who Albee noted was modeled after George Washington, ultimately realizes the truism of another American president, *the only thing we have to fear is fear itself,* a pronouncement that was sorely needed, and maybe forgotten, in the United States during the Cold War.

In an attempt to describe reality, George and Martha, I contend, play Wittgensteinian "language-games." The "language-games" show how words or concepts have many different meanings. And this is another reason why Albee so *values language*. To echo George's love of history, language is special because in its *use*, not in its idealistic scientific form, language captures "the surprise, the multiplexity, the sea-changing rhythm." What is also important here is that the *use* of reality for George and Martha serves different purposes for each one of them. Martha uses these "language-games" to describe a reality that would break George, who uses "language-games" to describe the reality of their "son," which should he prove successful (which we know he does), should, in turn, break Martha.

The tension of the play is that the "son" represents the metaphorical difficulties over issues of principles of verification (of the logical positivists). The climax of the play is George's utterance of the "performative," "our . . . son . . . is . . . DEAD!" The play, after an initial reaction by Martha, quietly dies down and the realization that reality must be described as it is (via analytic philosophy), and not how it should be (via logical positivism), is quickly realized. (Metaphorically speaking, the emergence of analytic philosophy that resulted from the death of logical positivism nicely mirrors the emergence of a new hopeful era in George and Martha's lives at the end of the play that resulted from the death of their "son.")

I am in no way suggesting that Albee consciously wrote this play with the history of analytic philosophy in mind. That would be highly doubtful, even given the fact that George calls Nick quite a epistemologically philosophical contradiction: that Nick might believe in a sort of "pragmatic idealism" (92), which alerts the audience to the fact that Albee at least knew the two opposing viewpoints in one of the debates (see Chapter 2) between empiricism and rationalism. However, given the fact that the ideas from analytic philosophy were in the air at the time, and since this play is so dominated by *language*, these debates are very helpful in giving us a *language* to describe the reality of the play.

That is not to say that the contextual history was not relevant: very much the opposite, in fact. In *Viginira Woolf?*, Albee does one very important thing: he displaces the fear of the here and now (i.e., the Cold War) into a battle between a terrifying future and a (possibly nostalgic) past.⁶⁰ With this, George becomes a very problematic character. Clearly, Nick represents some dystopic version of a future Communist takeover, while George's bohemian rhapsody about his love of the unpredictability of history is supposed to help the audience see George's humanistic side. While threat of a world war was in people's minds, Albee actually creates a more dystopic picture than his current situation (at least from the standpoint of "cultural unease"): the United States in the early 1960s saw the emergence of some type of counter-culture and beginnings of a cultural revolution, and certainly literary revolution, of which Albee was a major part. While the audience expects the young counter-culture to displace the conservative status quo made up of an older generation, the young generation of *Virginia Woolf?*, as represented by Nick and Honey, is more conservative than their seniors, George and Martha.⁶¹ One clue as to why this may be comes from Albee, himself. In Albee's 1962 essay "Some Notes on Nonconformity," Albee attacks the fact that "everybody these days is nonconformist, or pretends to be (conformity has become a dirty word)," and that people try to "possess" the "fashionable far-out," which, in turn, makes the intellectual conversation of the day "terribly conformist."⁶² Read in light of Albee's essay, *Virginia Woolf?* is a warning that a "fashionable" counter-culture will be just as stifling, conformist, and dependent on the status quo as "a race of scientists and mathematicians, each dedicated to and working for the greater glory of the super-civilization."⁶³ And therefore, the greatest threat to our society, Albee claims, is not from Communists and their nukes from other countries, but from the threat that comes from inside our very own culture.

As Albee suggests that the word "conformity" has become a "dirty word," Albee displaces the fear of conformity into the scientism of biology, where the search for truth signifies an almost-Fascist ideal. The science of language in logical positivism can almost be seen as a parallel movement to the literary modernist trend of symbolism and the search for one truth. Albee, maybe most evidently in *Zoo Story*, and maybe not in a necessarily postmodern fashion, certainly dismantles the theory of one truth. Returning to the problem of George in the play, while George claims to love the unpredictability of history, George is the most exacting character in terms of seeking a very strict version of truth. George constantly corrects the others on their grammar, zeroing in on a precise definition. These are the "language-games" that George is constantly playing. (It is after all George who basically initiates the "games" in the play, or at least pronounces the fact that they are playing them.)

While it is common to think of *Waiting for Godot* as a play about two men who talk the entire play, as it relates to the title of this book, *Words, Space, and the Audience,* the preoccupation of philosophy at the time and of *Virginia Woolf?* is the *play* specifically of *words*. While in *Godot* the stage directions and staging are sparse, there is tremendous weight attached to the few instances where space and gesture, while momentary, overtake the play. On the other hand, in *Virginia Woolf?,* while the play is more or less a "living room" drama in a realistic setting ("*The living room of a house on the campus of a small New England college*"), there is much less of a focus on the space and gestures in the play and how they are used by the director/actors and the audience to generate meaning. The doorbell and the toy gun (which I will return to in the conclusion), for example, are maybe the most important elements of the set (if you can even relegate the doorbell to the set). The focus on *words* in *Virginia Woolf?* is a sign of the times (i.e., from the philosophical conversations in the early 1960s).

As mentioned earlier, while Albee engages with the question of existence that occupied the minds of intellectuals in the 1950s, Albee raises these questions at the beginning of the play only to show that the conversation has moved past the question of existence that so dominated the newspaper headlines in Paris in 1952. A decade later, Albee asserts in his essay "Which Theater is the Absurd One?" that, should he even be labeled as such (for unless the label of the Theatre of the Absurd is understood as "doing something of the same thing in vaguely similar ways at approximately the same time" then the "labeling itself will be more absurd than the label"), maybe The Theatre of the Absurd is on its way out: "Or at least it is undergoing change. All living organisms undergo constant change."[64] One way, I suggest his theatre changes, at least with *Virginia Woolf?* is by paying homage to his frontrunner, Beckett, through taking up the question of existence, but then Albee is "moving in his own direction," as Albee also says of Pinter: "Harold

Pinter, for example, could not have written *The Caretaker* had Samuel Beckett not existed, but Pinter is, nonetheless, moving in his own direction."[65] While opening the play with these questions of existence which, in a sense, the audience probably expected in 1962 after a few years of Beckett, Genet, and Pinter dominating the stage, Albee does this to orient the audience in one direction, only to spend the rest of the play contradicting or moving past the audience's initial bearings in order to disorient the audience into making sense of the situation presented in front of them.

Early on *Virginia Woolf?*, after a laborious conversation between the fighting couple, George and Martha, where Martha is trying to figure out the name of a movie, George says he is tired. Martha responds, "... you haven't *done* anything all day..."[66] A few lines later, Martha expands upon her statement: "You didn't *do* anything; you never *do* anything; you never *mix*. You just sit around and *talk*."[67] Here we see the same tension between being and doing that was thoroughly discussed in *Godot*. As if just talking and George's lack of action are signs of being nonexistent, shortly after, Martha suggests his nonexistence: "I swear... if you existed I'd divorce you..."[68] To Martha, the fact that George does not *do*, equates with George not existing. Furthermore, Martha states, "I can't even see you..."[69] While understanding existence through *seeing* and the effects somebody's actions (what one *does*) have on reality are empirical ways of understanding the world, these statements, rather, can suggest Martha's inability to understand her reality empirically, as her empirical method for understanding existence is not able to adequately explain George's existence. For the men of the play, George and Nick, carrying out their two disciplines (history and biology, respectively), at least how they are described in the play, are empirical and precise endeavors; the women in this play, Martha and Honey, on the other hand, lead lives mostly in the mind, forming little basis for their conceptions of reality based upon detailed observation.

Even though the entire play can be said to hinge on the *existence* of the "son," Albee quickly declares that this is not the question of *Virginia Woolf?* The first "performative" in the play (since the statement is neither true nor false, but is associated with an action) "O.K. O.K. Vanish" (and in the next line she leaves, "*Practically dragging* HONEY *out with her*") is almost a shout from Albee that says the conversations since *Godot* have changed and that Albee, himself, is "performatively" killing off the questions that occupied *Godot*.[70] With the "son," Albee is clearly playing around with the existence of the offstage presence (e.g., Godot in *Waiting for Godot*). It becomes awfully apparent by the end of the play that the "son" never existed in this play in order to discuss questions of existence, but to juxtapose the "son's" *presence in the absent* with what is *absent in the present* (i.e., the love in George and Martha's marriage), which is a fully comprehended description of the reality of the here and now.

To return to beginning of the play, *Virginia Woolf?* begins immediately with a very subtle Wittgensteinian hybrid "case" and "language-game" (the first of many examples in the play), as Martha tries to figure out which movie the expression "What a dump!" came from, after saying it when she "*looks about the room.*"[71] The first pronunciation of the phrase, refers to the context of the room, playing off of the staging, "*Set in darkness,*" while the second time she says it, she "*Imitates Bette Davis.*"[72] While Martha's descriptions of the movie that follow may seem insignificant, with each added bit of information, the reality of the film she is referring to, and thus the context and meaning of the phrase ("What a dump!"), changes: first, it is a movie about a woman who "gets peritonitis" and is "married to Joseph Cotton or something"; second, the woman in the movie wants to go to Chicago because she is in love with an actor with a scar; third, she is so sick she cannot put on lipstick but goes to Chicago anyway; fourth, she is a housewife who buys things and comes home to Joseph Cotton, to a modest living room and house; fifth, she is married to Joseph Cotton, and when she comes home with groceries and puts them down, she says, "What a dump!" The manner in which Martha tells the story does not (necessarily) appear to be in chronological order. While these are subtle shifts in the overall plot, these short descriptions connote different stories. Therefore, as the context from which the expression "What a dump!" comes from keeps changing, the meaning of the expression changes with each subtle shift of the story.

With Martha looking about the room while first saying "What a dump!" the audience immediately sees George and Martha's residence, and metaphorically their lives and relationship, in such a manner. And this play is largely about this. But even more so, this is a play where revelation through language constantly changes our image of George and Martha. We get their story, and, of course, the story of their "son" in bits and pieces. But the story of the "son" changes, too, ever so subtly (the best example of the subtlety being when they discuss his eye color). And this is why the seemingly insignificant opening "case" and "language-game" are so important. Besides setting up the theme of zeroing in on a truer description of reality, the audience, in this opening scene, also sees how the two operate. On one hand, Martha races through the story, while George, on the other hand, slows it down, bogging her down in the details. When Martha says that Bette Davis is "married to Joseph Cotton or something," George corrects her grammar: "Some*body*." George's attention to detail gets in the way of Martha's attempt at brushing over the important facts. This pattern gets replicated throughout the entire play.

But there is a notable departure from this pattern. When George is discussing his own history, he tends to omit the details of the past: for example, when Martha fills in the details about George's history in the History Department and how he never lived up to his father-in-law's expectations. George does display some dislike for the strict precision of language. George turns attention away from himself and turns things the unpleasant into stories. While for much of the play George treats language like the empirically oriented logical positivists in language's necessity for precision, George's "performantive" utterances are a signal that George is starting to see the limitations of the scientism of language. Given the fact that the gun George fires in the play is a toy, the performative utterance of murder, "You're dead! Pow! You're dead!" (57), foreshadows George's "performative" of arguably actual (metaphorical) murder when he pronounces, "our ... son ... is ... DEAD!"

As I wrote earlier, in many ways *Virginia Woolf?* is a purely psychological case study. With George and Martha's inability to be immortalized through progeny, Martha, especially (since without a job, without a particular thing to be defined by other than "housewife" and not "mother"), displays a fear of isolation and death. In other ways, however, the play is an epistemological Gordian Knot. On one hand, empiricism is displayed both as a mode of scientism (with Nick) and as humanistic (with George). On the other hand, rationalism is exacting at finding the truth (with

George) and useless without forms of empiricism (with Martha and Honey).

Even though I wrote earlier that this play is largely about *words,* the toy gun is very important in this play for three reasons. (1) The audience experiences the terrifying nature of not understanding the meaning or context behind George's actions. Without the audience having knowledge that this is a toy, the gun (a weapon) and its use (killing) first connote violence; then when it is realized that it is a toy, the gun (being a toy) and its use (playing) connote fun. The audience viscerally experiences a stunning reversal once the meaning and context behind George's actions are known. First, total dread; second, relief; and third, a chuckle over making a big deal over what was nothing. As our perception of reality shifts, so too does our understanding of it. Not a "language-game," the firing of the toy gun is a "prop-game." (2) As discussed before, the firing of the toy gun foreshadows the killing of the "son." This, of course, is a brilliant dramatic technique. (3) The firing of the toy gun allows the accompaniment of the performative utterance of "You're dead! Pow! You're dead!" Being a "performative" utterance, the above expression (which is so commonly uttered by children when playing with toy guns) performs a very real action: it "kills." But, of course, this "killing" is only make-believe. So "You're dead" is both true (your make-believe self is now dead) and false (you are not dead). So it is an unusual "performative" in that it is *not* neither true nor false (with a statement that is neither true nor false contradicting the assertion of the logical positivists that a statement must be either true or false), but, instead, it is *both* true and false (which still contradicts the assertion of the logical positivists).

Charles Isherwood and Katherine E. Kelly review two productions that suggest that George is much more of the central character.[73] Isherwood, reviewing the Steppenwolf 2010 production with Tracy Letts (George), suggests that this production is much more about "George's stealthy journey from apparently passive victim to merciless aggressor," and the ultimate liberator of both he and Martha.[74] And Kelly suggests that under Albee's direction in a 1990 production in College Station, Texas, that the central crux of the play is the "son-myth and its exorcism," through Albee's attempt, "to make and interpret history as a record of male conflict and concord."[75]

In such a way, I suggest that the movement with George's use of language may be one of the central issues in the play. George starts the play using language for precision, especially when it comes to discussing either things with Martha or things about Martha. Then, George, as represented by the "performative" utterances, begins to see how language is actually used, while not necessarily having to be precise. And finally, George moves past even the conversations of the analytic philosophers to the conversation that recently reached English speaking audiences with the translation of *Homo Ludens* in 1955: George understands play and make-believe, the power to play with language and create a new reality, but one that is used to understand reality even better. While earlier in the play, Nick comes to understand how George operates when the two are alone and George brings up Martha's stepmother and the two agree on how the story about the stepmother may or may not be true, with "All truth being relative" to George at the end of the play,[76] George has come to understand the glory of fiction to shed light on reality.

Conclusion

Returning to the epigraph that opened this chapter, Martha is still *afraid* at the very end of the play. What is Martha afraid of? While it can be argued that it is simply hard to face the truth, to face a truth that neither ever wanted (i.e., that George and Martha could not and cannot have a child), maybe this, ultimately, has more to do with a clash between the empirical and the rational in the face of an uncertain personal (and historical) moment. Martha is not a historian and, thus, while Martha can rationalize that their uncertain future will be better now that they face the truth, Martha does not have that empirical evidence of previous experience. George, however, being a historian, has studied the "sea-changing rhythm of... history." George is not just familiar with the seismic shifts in history, but he actually enjoys the knowledge that history is unpredictable, calling its "unpredictability" "glorious." Thus, George ends the play with the playful lines of "Who's afraid of Virginia Woolf," as George sees their own unpredictable future as something "glorious." And while Martha's fear is certainly palpable at the end of the play, the confidence, knowledge, and love that George displays in the final scene suggests to the audience that everything will be okay; that the best way to approach an uncertain future (as an uncertain future was a sentiment shared by most in the audience when the play premiered) is to acknowledge, with sometimes brutal honesty, our past and our present, not what it should be, but what the way it really *is*.

Conclusion: The Epistemological Quandary over Improvisation, Impermanence, and Lack of a Script in Performance Art—An Interview with Coco Fusco

As we have seen that matters of philosophy have an interesting way of weaving in and out of history, it makes for a very nice coincidence (or maybe explanation) that J. L. Austin's theory of "performatives," found in the posthumously published *How to Do Things with Words* (1962), was the result of a series of 12 lectures Austin gave at Harvard University in 1955: the very same year that Johan Huizinga's seminal *Homo Ludens: A Study of the Play-Element in Culture* first appeared in English (seminal, especially, to performance studies). Because of this, I can say one of two things about this conclusion: the subject of performance studies with regard to this book is an afterthought, or, in the exact opposite manner, this entire book culminates with this conclusion.

This conclusion muses on one of the major epistemological questions inherent in much of performance art: if (as a huge generality) there is often no "script," per se—that is, no stable, unchanging text—can our understanding of performance art *only* be based upon a subjective phenomenology? In understanding performance art, do we all have to come to the same conclusion that George does in *Who's Afraid of Virginia Woolf?*: "All truth being relative"?[1] As much as I would like to be able to answer this question for performance art in general, that is a task for another entire book. However, I hope to shed some light on this question via a specific performance artist, through an interview with Coco Fusco. My reason for choosing to interview Fusco (as opposed to other performance artists) was a very personal one. Coco Fusco and Guillermo Gómez-Peña's *Undiscovered Amerindians* (as documented in the film *The Couple in the Cage*, which Fusco also codirected) was the first piece of performance art that I studied in graduate school. In a sense, this performance (or the video of it, rather) provided my foundation to what I think of when I think of performance art. And since this is an academic book, Fusco, who is also an academic, speaks through a nice lens (as both an artist and scholar) in which to view performance (or, at least, her performances).

INTERVIEW[2]

> *BENNETT*: In terms of the role of the improvisation, what kind of "script" do you create for performances, and I'm guessing that it will vary?
>
> *FUSCO*: Yes, when I have done performances that involved a lot of tech, like multimedia, like compositing, relying on technicians, I need a script because the technician has to be able to follow a script and I have to stay on the script because the technician has to be able to execute his or her operations and it has to match whatever is happening on the stage. So pieces like *The Incredible Disappearing Woman* or even *A Room of One's Own, New World Border*, which I worked on with Guillermo Gómez-Peña, they were scripted to the word. When I have done performances that were not in black box, they don't always involve tech, there is a little bit more flexibility. When you rely on others—when you are interacting with others—you always have to have some kind of agreement prior to the beginning of the work as to what we think is going to happen, or we create a set of terms and then the variables—what the audience may do, as in the case of *The Cage* piece—but we agree on a certain set of terms prior to the performance. With *Dolores from 10 to 10,* which was a 12 hour

performance in which neither I nor Ricardo could break character, we said every hour there is going to be a set of goals. We have 12 goals in this, which is something of a semi-scripted improvisational structure. Each hour is going to be marked by a different goal. The goal of that one hour scene might be, Coco has to get to the bathroom, or Ricardo is going to eat in front of Coco and make her feel bad, or Coco is going to destroy the computer. Within that we start to develop an interaction in which we have talked through, but you don't know every single detail.

In the case of *Bare Life Study*, we had a plan, we knew what we were going to do. I rehearsed with the students who were with me and carried it out. The variable was that we didn't know what the consulate was going to do with us, but we knew what we were going to try to get through on a particular time period. Part of this was that I had 40 or 50 students with me, and I had technicians, and photo journalist and we had to coordinate the drivers and the chauffeurs, everything. And the production has to be orchestrated so that everybody knew what to do. Even when I am working myself I have to have a plan in my mind. So if I did *Votos* on my own, I still have to be in the space at a particular time, so it is never a total free-for-all. There are people who allow audience to structure the activity a lot more. I do allow audience to interact with me in many instances but I have a plan on my head.

BENNETT: Right, that in some ways answers my question about preparation. It sounds like you prepare for the possible outcomes that you foresee.

FUSCO: There are a bunch of things that I want to do in a performance and I have to go through it. I don't just go, I going to just stand there and whatever happens happens, no. I am doing this piece based on this idea, or I am doing this piece that is a simulation of what I imagined is going to happen in a factory, or I have a script. There is always some structure in my mind that is governing what I am doing.

BENNETT: My last question about improvisation, though, of course, some performances are improvised or some are scripted or thought out before, is what are the most difficult moments when you have to improvise?

FUSCO: Well, not knowing what to do, I suppose, would be the most difficult thing. Or overreacting to an unanticipated situation would be another difficult moment.

BENNETT: Examples? Do you have any specific time you remember in one performance that you were like "wow, what do I do?"

FUSCO: In many performances, improvisation is what you need to be able to cover a mistake. I had a piece where the technician completely screwed up. He wasn't doing what he was supposed to be doing. In the moment I kind of froze because he is not doing what he is supposed to be doing: what is going on, how I cover this? I needed to figure out a solution and it just did not come to me right away. Once when we were doing *The Cage* piece, I got sick, I had a stomach virus and was throwing up, so I tried to leave the cage to throw up, and my temperature dropped so I was very cold. And I was kind of shivering with a blanket on me and I know that Guillermo was starting to get frustrated because I was running out of ideas as to what to do and to cover to my illness. There are situations like that that are difficult. I told my students, if you are not really good at what you do and don't have the experience, don't try to improvise. Improvisation doesn't mean it is easier because you don't have to plan. Improvisation is much more difficult than planning. Improvisation requires foreknowledge of a variety of possibilities that would work in a given situation. The way that you phenomenologically experience time in a performance situation is very different than in real life. You cannot rely on your faculties functioning in the same way. It is like a musician, if you can't play violin you can't improvise. You can make a mess, but that is not improvisation.

BENNETT: Let's move to "interaction" with an "audience,"[3] as well, because I think they are flexible terms. In general, how do you, say, "interact" with the audience, and I understand it will depend on the performance, as well?

FUSCO: Yes, sometimes I interact with the audience in a very direct way where I am physically in proximity to them, or asking them to be part of the work in a very direct way. My sense of things, particularly with people who didn't anticipate being an audience, they are not going to put up with a lot of aggression. I am better off being ludic and light about it, and trying to make it seem like fun. There is a sense of annoyance for some people in having the fourth wall broken. With *A Room of One's Own*, where I addressed the audience but I had script and I didn't have to bring anybody else on the stage, and I knew I was making them look at things that were not pleasant, I could evoke their presence. I can listen for their body language and verbal responses to what I was doing. But there really wasn't a reason for me to go beyond that.

BENNETT: You talked about the observers as sometimes they don't know they are in the audience? How do you consider observers, are they an audience?

FUSCO: If people buy tickets for a theater play, they have chosen to attend. It is not a surprise that they find themselves before of work. It is not unanticipated. They want to know what are they getting and they have an idea of what they are getting when they come in. They might be disappointed but they had an idea and they chose to be there. And that is very different from coming upon me in a public place, coming upon me in a shopping mall, bumping into me at a big art event without any announced performance. Then you have to deal with people who are unwilling audiences. They didn't choose to be part of the performance. They didn't choose to attend, they didn't choose to experience it, and you are going to get a wider range of reactions as a result of that.

BENNETT: How do you imagine words and space interacting. I will clarify that, for your performances that are site specific, how does the site specificity affect the words you use? [. . .] In, for example, *Rites of Passage*, there was funneling, people were being funneled in and funneled out, not just being in South Africa, I'm considering the physical space. Were you considering, we have this physical space where people are funneling in and funneling out, and would that affect the words you chose? For example, if you are in a cramped space, do you talk to people differently? Or as a "passport control," when there were moments that seemed confined, did the actual physical space in that long hallway, did that affect how you spoke to people, or visa versa?

FUSCO: I couldn't talk with most people during the performance. There were hundreds and hundreds of them there. When you are in a chaotic environment like that, I just struggled to stay in character and continue to set out what I was trying to do. But I wasn't trying to address all of them as a crowd.

BENNETT: The space led for a chaotic environment. Going back to the idea of improvisation, and understanding the possible outcomes, would you say in that instance was the space and the words you used the product of the kind of the chaos that ensued from that space?

FUSCO: We planned what we could we planned. The people who were working with me, we had a plan of what we were going to say. We had no idea how many people were going to show up and once we were there we were just trying to hold it together and to stay in character because there were irate South Africans who were irate because they had to wait and irate because they did not like the subject matter, they did not want the apartheid thrown in their faces, so there was a lot of kind of damage control to try to how to keep the performance going in that environment.

When you are in the middle of this, the conceptual is not in the foreground of your mind. It is the practical, how do I get through this? And that's all! I have 500 people in a hall screaming. I can't worry about anything other than how do I get through this. The same with *The Cage* piece, we had 30,000 people passing through the Natural History Museum in Washington, DC, on any given weekend, when you have those kinds of crowds, you just work on staying focused.

BENNETT: With the advent of technology, a lot of your earlier works were not recorded on video, right? I see more and more of your works on video now.

FUSCO: There were videos that weren't based on performance I chose not to make a video of stuff because it was very much a live piece and some performance videos really work, some really don't; a piece was not going to look good as a video unless I shot it in a studio and did it as a video and I have the forces. With the performances that I did in Cuba, I didn't have the technical resources in the 90s to get professional cameras to videotape it, so I have photographs as a document of those pieces. A lot of these choices are not aesthetic choices; it is about time and money. It takes a lot of money to produce a video or a performance well and I would rather not make them if they are going be bad or wait until I can make one.

BENNETT: My question with the video is, when you know you are doing a video (and this is a more specific question for *Undiscovered Amerindians*), who in your head is the "audience"? Is the audience the onlookers—the people who are actually at the live performance—or, in a sense, those watching the video, *The Couple in the Cage?*

FUSCO: I often tell people when I discuss the video, they are a very different type of audience than the audience that was there, looking at the video, knowing what it is versus the people who were there looking at something without knowing what it is and it changes everything about how you approach the work and how you respond emotionally to the work. It is easy for people watching the video to laugh at the audience, but they were not there. It is a different feeling when you come across something where people are acting in a very strange way, you have a docent in front of you lying like crazy, saying that it is something that you don't think it is. So I don't underestimate for a moment how much of an advantage the video audience has. They heard the story before they saw the video.[4] And the video is not going to implicate them the way that the piece made people feel put against a wall in the Amerindian performance because there was nowhere to escape to.

CONCLUSION

BENNETT: Why document?

FUSCO: Performance doesn't really exist unless you document it these days. We are not in the 60s anymore when somebody's hip story about what they saw would fly. I need to circulate my work beyond the context of the performance. I need to provide material for archive. I was very interested in the way the video looked in *Dolores* after the streaming performance, and I decide to make a video installation out of it. The same with videotaping the training with the interrogators. I didn't know if I was going to make a video, but when I saw what I had, I wanted to make a video out of it. I do engage artistically in both areas. I don't need to be a purist about performances only live because I am also interested in mediated not just liveness and the effect of transmitting performed experience through different forms of media. There are pictures of my performances, videos of my performances, and I don't feel like that is a betrayal in any way of the spirit of the performance.

BENNETT: What is "lost," though, in the documentation?

FUSCO: The physical and psychological experience of being there with it. It's not the same thing. To be honest, 99.9 percent of the critical writing that has been done on my work by scholars has been produced by people who have never attended a performance of mine. I cannot change the reality that scholars prefer to work with dead material, and they tend to work with material that has already been legitimated by somebody else. I am sure there are a few art historians out there who do go see performances, but my experience has been that the overwhelming majority of scholars and critics who are interested in the work, are only interested after it happens and only look at the documents. And in some cases I find it highly suspect. And sometimes they come to me 20 years later and there is nothing else they can work with. But I do find it highly suspect that there are some historians that if they just don't like the idea of it, will trash it based just upon the idea of it. I am like, you weren't there, you didn't see it. What are you talking about? With what authority can you make a claim about what the performance is if you didn't see it?

BENNETT: When you do have a site-specific performance, would you say that it is a "fleeting event"? I mean you do have ways to document it, but in that time that space, is there something "lost"?

FUSCO: I think there is an obsession with liveness as in pieces with Peggy Phelan. I do think there is something very pleasurable, very particular. My last experience with *Bare Life Study* was great in the moment, but when photo journalists who were all there taking pictures and sending them out into the media, it acquired an entire life of its own, a new life, beyond the moment.[5] And it's just as important to me as what happened in the moment. The same with the *Amerindian* piece, it exists as a legend because of what happened afterwards because we made a postcard and we sent it out to people and we told this crazy story. And then rumors started to spread. And then we made the video and thousands and thousands of students have seen the video and written papers about it. So it takes on a different life because of its mediation. It wasn't all about selling it [...] The point of the mediation wasn't to bring more audience back to the performance, whereas the publicity machine of a museum is a very calculated attempt to bring more audience back.

BENNETT: What is permanent and what is impermanent? You said that pieces take on a life of their own. Even if you were there, there is something there. Honestly, I was 12 years old when you did *Undiscovered Amerindians,* but it "exists" for me, it exists in a different reality. [...] What, then, is permanent even if someone wasn't there? How do you see your pieces remaining permanent, or in what way are they permanent?

FUSCO: The documentation is there. My chronicle is there. Guillermo has made many written comments about the experience, as well. The history of discussion surrounding it is there, as well.[6] One of the ironies is that people did not like what we did when we did it. It was not a popular piece. It wasn't an instant hit. We were benefiting from a certain mainstream cultural institution interest in multiculturalism. They were giving funding to work with people like us. And it was the year of the Quincentenary. So you can make an argument for the topicality of the work, so that was advantageous. But it was not a critical success at the onset. In a way, we got a lot of invitations because Guillermo just got a MacArthur. It wasn't until much later, that the work proved itself to be resilient and it proved itself to have staying power. Some of that was because we made an effort to create effective documentation. And some of it was because I went out on the road. It became a point that I wanted to make as an artist and as a performance artist. I was going to control the life of that work and make sure it remained in people's minds. I spent two years going around the country and the world, showing and showing and showing the documentation, talking about the work, to make sure that it would be institutionalized. The publicity power of the '93 biennial really got the piece into the history of art. It wasn't the reaction in the moment.

Conclusion: Performance as an Alternative to Being versus Doing

While I am tempted to "read" my interview with Coco Fusco, I have decided to let her words speak for themselves. It should be clear to the reader, without my "reading" of the interview, that Fusco and I discussed many epistemological issues in performance art directly discussed in this book. Fusco's answers should make it clear that performance art both complicates and clarifies some of the epistemological issues that are omnipresent in the theatre: while Fusco repeats many times the need to "stay in character," which is a typical requisite of "traditional" theatre actors, the Performer-Audience and Actor-Audience Relationships, for example, are much more complex in performance art.

To end, I would like to indirectly discuss the issues Fusco brought up by addressing the epistemology of performance as it relates to understanding people. Here, I would like to return to where I began: Shakespeare's *Hamlet*. As I introduced this book, Hamlet contemplates, through the juxtaposition of Hamlet's monologue and the Gravedigger's speech, the *being versus doing* debate that has permeated this book. With Hamlet—with the question, "To be or not to be"—we see one side of the epistemological debate; with the Gravedigger's pronouncement of action, we see the other. The context of when the two minds meet is in a graveyard. The focus is on death. Here, the Gravedigger's suggestion rings true: while Alexander the Great (who, being a student of Aristotle) ends up essentially like all of the other skulls—"Alexander died, Alexander was buried, Alexander returneth to dust" (251)—Alexander was Alexander because of what he accomplished. But Shakespeare considers something else. Shakespeare throws his own weight into the debate and contemplates how "performance" totally transforms and complicates the question of epistemology. For after all, the *plot* of *Hamlet* (i.e., the future course of action) hinges on two performances: the performance of the play and Hamlet and Laertes' public duel.

Appearing between *Homo Ludens* and *How to Do Things with Words,* Erving Goffman's *The Presentation of Self in Everyday Life* (1959) discusses the social actor and the fact that humans constantly perform in different social situations. Bauman's "consciousness" of doubleness" also is noteworthy here: a performance is a self-aware performance and a performance *for* someone. We must also think back about the Performer-Actor Relationship discussed in the introduction of this book. And we must consider the role of performance concerning Hamlet. When Hamlet speaks with his best friend, Horatio, at the end of the play, there is no sign of madness: for he is not being observed by others (other than Horatio, whom he trusts). However, when Hamlet suspects or knows he has an audience, his madness comes out.

Hamlet's two different selves put the spotlight on my earlier discussion of *insincere performance* and the Performer-Audience Relationship versus the Actor-Audience Relationship. At what point, if it does, does an "actor" become a "performer," and visa versa? At what point, if it does, does an *insincere performance* become *sincere?* Another way to ask the same question is, even though Shen Teh, in Brecht's *The Good Person of Szechwan,* is forced to adopt a role not her own, does the constant performance of Shui Ta rub off on who Shen Teh is? Does Algy's Bunburying somehow overtake and become part of Algy? How much of Fusco's planned improvisation is a performance (versus how much is acted)? Especially in matters of performance (versus in matters of acting), does one become one's performance? Since everyone performs all of the time, the question becomes, to rephrase Bert O. States' line, is there a ghost of the performance in the actor, a ghost of our performances in us?

NOTES

INTRODUCTION

1. Gay McAuley, *Space in Performance: Making Meaning in the Theatre* (Ann Arbor: The University of Michigan Press, 2000) 107.
2. William Shakespeare, *Hamlet,* eds. Barbara A. Mowat and Paul Werstine (New York: Washington Square Press, 1992) 127.
3. Ibid. 239.
4. It should be noted that Hamlet is saying this as a prince and the Gravedigger is saying this as a peasant. Of course, the *idea* of *being a prince* is greater than the personhood of any one person. Therefore, why would Hamlet not want to be defined by an essentialist view of being (and princehood)? On the other hand, the Gravedigger would never want to be defined essentially through his birth or being: he would be condemned to *being a peasant.* The Gravedigger would much rather let his *actions* define him, for his *being a peasant* can never change.

    Henry James brilliantly describes the psychology behind this in *The Golden Bowl.* Amerigo, a previously cash-poor Italian prince, arguably, married Maggie Verver (maybe subconsciously) for her father's money. Charlotte is an American, who before her marriage to Maggie's father, Adam Verver, had no money. Charlotte and Amerigo, who knew each other before either met the Ververs and could not marry because neither had money, have an affair throughout much of the novel. Here, Charlotte speaks to Amerigo:

    > "Passive then—not active. My romance is that, if you want to know, I've been all day on the town. Literally on the town—isn't that what they call it? I know how it feels." After which, as if breaking off, "And you, have you never been out?" she asked.

    > He still stood there with his hands in his pockets. "What should I have gone out for?"

"Oh, what should people in our case do anything for? But you're wonderful, all of *you*—you know how to live. We're clumsy brutes, we others, beside you—we must always be 'doing' something..."
(Henry James, *The Golden Bowl,* ed. Virginia Llewellyn Smith [Oxford: Oxford University Press, 2009], 221)

5. This paragraph was sparked by the "Observer's Talk" by Rustom Bharucha at the International Federation of Theatre Research conference in Osaka, Japan, on August 12, 2011. Bharucha was discussing the difficulty of observing a conference because he suggests that it is a panoptic and an exclusive endeavor.
6. This expansion of understand calls to mind the work of Hans-Georg Gadamer's theory of hermeneutics and his talk of expanding one's "horizons": see Hans-Georg Gadamer, *Truth and Method,* 2nd ed. (London: Continuum, 2011).
7. Antonin Artaud, "The Theatre of Cruelty," *The Theory of the Modern Stage: An Introduction to Modern Theatre and Drama,* ed. Eric Bentley (Middlesex: Penguin Books, 1970) 55.
8. Ibid. 58.
9. Ibid.
10. Dominique D. Fisher, *Staging of Language and Language(s) of the Stage: Marllarmé's poëme critique and Artaud's poetry-minus-text* (New York: Peter Lang: 1994) 86.
11. Ibid. 84.
12. Ibid. 86.
13. Ibid. 89–90.
14. Ibid. 91.
15. Ibid. 92.
16. Ibid.
17. Ibid. 96.
18. Ibid. 99.
19. Ferdinand de Saussure, *Course in General Linguistics,* Ed. Charles Bally and Albert Sechehaye, Trans. Roy Harris (Chicago: Open Court, 2000) 67.
20. Telory W. Davies, "Performance Review of *Rhinoceros,*" *Theatre Journal* 54.4 (December 2002): 646.
21. Bert O. States, *Great Reckonings in Little Rooms: On the Phenomenology of the Theater* (Berkeley: University of California Press, 1985) 34.
22. Ibid. 46.
23. Ibid. 55.
24. Ibid. 56.
25. Ibid. 61.

26. F. S. C. Northrop, "Leibniz's Theory of Space," *Journal of the History of Ideas* 7.4 (October 1946): 437.
27. States.
28. A. D. Smith, "Space and Sight," *Mind* 109.435 (July 2000): 483–484.
29. Ibid. 511.
30. Ibid. 512.
31. Tracy C. Davis and Thomas Postlewait, "Theatricality: An Introduction," *Theatricality,* ed. Tracy C. Davis and Thomas Postlewait (Cambridge: Cambridge University Press, 2004) 5.
32. Ibid.
33. Ibid.
34. Ibid. 8.
35. Ibid. 13.
36. Ibid.
37. Ibid.
38. Ibid. 14.
39. Ibid. 14–15.
40. Ibid. 15.
41. Ibid. 17.
42. Ibid. 19.
43. Ibid. 20.
44. Ibid. 26.
45. Ibid. 27.
46. Ibid. 28.
47. Ibid. 29.
48. Ibid. 33.
49. However, a Kantian might disagree and say that it is not the "concept" is universal but the mental abilities that allow for acting. Kant's theory of "pure concepts" suggests that we understand concepts like cause and effect because our minds are equipped to organize the sensory information we receive in such a manner.

CHAPTER 1

1. William Shakespeare, *Hamlet* (New York: Washington Square Press, 1992), 127.
2. This thesis is playing off of (1) Joseph Donohue's idea: "The question must therefore be asked, what was Wilde doing when he set out to write a play not only in a tongue but in a form not really his own?" ("*Salome* and the Wildean Art of Symbolist Theater," *Modern Drama* 37.1 (Spring 1994): 86), and (2) Jacqueline Vanhoutte's idea

that the characters are "mere mouthpieces for the language" ("*Salome's* Earnestness," *Text and Presentation* 13 (1992): 83).

3. Pauline Gregg, *A Social and Economic History of Britain: 1760–1965* (London: George G. Harrap & Co. Ltd, 1965) 367. According to Gregg, Britain did not stop being prosperous or eminent: rather, the economy was vulnerable and total wealth increased at a slower rate, especially compared to places like the United States and Germany (381).

4. Gregg 372.

5. The Imperial Empire was strengthened by the Imperial Federation League of 1884, a Colonial and Indian Exhibition of 1886, and a series of Colonial Conferences starting in 1887. While New Imperialism (which relied on strengthened ties with its colonies and the undeveloped lands of Africa) extended the life of British capitalism, it also paved the way for a second era of slavery, "in which the coloured peoples were brought in to arrest a decline which the white races alone were powerless to stem" (Gregg 376). At that time, Britain's foreign policy was largely thought of as isolationist, except concerning their colonies:

> It is customary to speak of the last twenty or thirty years of the nineteenth century as the period of "splendid isolation" in British foreign policy; but this is true only in a limited sense. The British certainly ceased to concern themselves with the Balance of Power in Europe; they supposed that it was self-adjusting. But they maintained close connexion with the continental Powers for the sake of affairs outside Europe, particularly in the Near East.
> (A. J. P. Taylor, *The Struggle for Mastery in Europe: 1848–1918* [London: Oxford University Press, 1974], 346.)

Britain tried to secure an alliance with Germany, but, ultimately, Britain went at it without an ally and settled on strengthening their navy to defend their imperial interests, which, ultimately, succeeded (Taylor 346–347).

6. Gregg 388.

7. Gregg 388 and 391. Soon after, a series of new political parties dotted the British political landscape: the Democratic Federation. The Democratic Federation, which was founded by a wealthy Radical who was influenced by Marx, desired universal suffrage, equal electoral districts, payment of Members, the abolition of the House of Lords, and triennial Parliaments. Some wanted the state to act in the interests of the working class with universal free education (with school feeding), a legal eight-hour day, state-aided housing plans, public work projects for the unemployed, the redemption of the national

debt, and a graduated taxation system to alleviate some of the burden for poor taxpayers (Gregg 392). The result of this was the revival of Socialism, which first expressed itself in the formation of new unions. The Socialist League (which split from the Democratic Federation) formed in 1884: "The Socialist League allied the gradualism of the Fabians with a disdain of the State characteristic of the Anarchists and with a belief in the revolution of heart and mind typical of the Christian and the artist" (Gregg 394).

The Fabian Society, formed in 1884, wanted a socialist state, not through revolution, but by gradual means: spreading their ideas and taking practical steps in local or national government to improve social conditions (Gregg 395–396). The Labour Party formed, in 1893 (and put 29 candidates forward in the 1895 General Election), when delegates from the Labour Clubs, the Democratic Federation, the Fabian Society, the Scottish Labour Party, and the trade unions elected (former Independent Socialist) Keir Hardie to represent them (Gregg 398).

8. Matthew Fforde, *Conservatism and Collectivism, 1886–1914* (Edinburgh: Edinburgh University Press, 1990) 41–42.
9. Fforde 42.
10. Frederick Copleston, *A History of Philosophy: Volume VIII: Modern Philosophy: Empiricism, Idealism, and Pragmatism in Britain and America* (New York: Image Books, 1966) 165.
11. Ibid. 168–169.
12. Ibid. 207.
13. For an unparalleled examination of Wilde's philosophical studies at Oxford, see Philip E. Smith II and Michael S. Helfand, "The Context of the Text," *Oscar Wilde's Oxford Notebooks: A Portrait of Mind in the Making,* ed. Philip E. Smith II and Michael S. Helfand (New York: Oxford University Press, 1989) 5–34. The entire book, not just this chapter, is illuminating and actual notes by Wilde from his notebooks are a gold mine for archival research. Furthermore, Joseph Bristow and Philip E. Smith II are currently editing a book for publication on a different notebook that Wilde wrote during his time at Oxford, entitled "Notebook on philosophy." Wilde, in this notebook, whose handwritten pages are very difficult to decipher (and, hence, why Bristow and Smith's book is so needed), devotes pages and pages to ideas that were at the forefront of the idealism versus empiricism/materialism debate. In this notebook, Wilde includes quotes from many of the principal philosophers that formed the backbones of British idealism and materialism: Plato, Aristotle, Bacon, Descartes, Locke, Kant, Hegel, Comte, Mill, Spinoza, and

Hume (Oscar Wilde, "[Notebook on philosophy]: 1874–1878," held at the William Andrews Clark Memorial Library, UCLA [Wilde W6721M3 N9113 [1876/8] Bound]).

For more about Wilde's time and study at Oxford see, Richard Ellmann, *Oscar Wilde* (New York: Alfred A. Knopf, 1988) 37–100; Richard Ellmann, *Oscar Wilde at Oxford* (Washington: Library of Congress, 1984); Peter Chapin, "Wilde at Oxford/Oxford Gone Wilde," *Reading Wilde: Querying Spaces* (New York: New York University Fales Library, 1995) 27–34; and Christopher Armitage, "Blue China and Blue Moods: Oscar Fashioning Himself at Oxford," *Oscar Wilde: The Man, His Writings, and His World*, ed. Robert N. Keane (New York: AMS Press, 2003) 15–24.

14. It would appear that Wilde was very close to Müller, as at least Müller seemed to take quite a liking to Wilde: " 'Max Müller loves him,' Lady Wilde wrote to a friend in 1875" (Smith and Helfand 9).
15. Smith and Helfand 14.
16. Ibid. 16.
17. Ibid. 14.
18. Ibid. 16–17.
19. For an in-depth examination of Wallace and Jowett's philosophy and Wilde's own view on their philosophies (based upon Wilde's own notes) see, Smith and Helfand 17–22.
20. Smith and Helfand 17.
21. Ibid.
22. Ibid. 33.
23. Oscar Wilde, "The Truth of Masks," *Intentions* (Amherst, NY: Prometheus Books, 2004) 263.
24. Smith and Helfand 32–33.
25. Oscar Wilde, *The Importance of Being Earnest and Other Plays*, ed. Peter Raby (Oxford: Oxford UP, 2008) 253.
26. For a further look at Wilde's dialectical turn, see Bruce Bashford, "Oscar Wilde: The Critic as Dialectician," *Visions and Revisions: Irish Writers in Their Time: Oscar Wilde*, ed. Jarlath Killeen (Dublin: Irish Academic Press, 2011) 113–135.
27. Thomas Wright, *Oscar's Books* (London: Chatto & Windus, 2008) 98.
28. Alvin Klein, "Theater: A Play for a Past Century, This One and the Next," *The New York Times* October 31, 1999: NJ12.
29. I draw this observation from theatre reviews over the past 20 or so years in *The New York Times*. Even though each of these productions had a slightly different emphasis, none particularly played the play in a new revelatory light: see Wilborn Hampton, "Review/Theater

'The Importance of Being Earnest,'" *The New York Times* March 18, 1990; Klein, "A Play for a Past Century"; Lawrence Van Gelder, "Theater Review: Wilde's Vitorian Wit Dumbed Down in Drag," *The New York Times* July 5, 2003; Caryn James, "A Thoroughly Modern Oscar and Algernon," *The New York Times* May 7, 2008; Naomi Siegel, "Redgrave Leads an 'Earnest' That Delights the Eye and Ear," *The New York Times* January 24, 2009; and Charles Isherwood, "Lady Bracknell is Back, With a Slightly Unladylike Air," *The New York Times* August 26, 2009.

30. Sara Freeman, "Performance Review of The Importance of Being Earnest, and Travesties," *Theatre Journal* 58.2 (May 2006): 356.
31. "The *Earnest* sets had the great benefit of encouraging an inventive physicality in the performance. The movement in the show refused to be confined by the verisimilitude of standing and sitting and pouring tea in drawing rooms and gardens... In act 3, the quartet of lovers... unleashed childlike playfulness as they eavesdropped on each other, hiding behind the furniture and rolling across the floor to elude detection. The vocal world of the play reflected this freedom, too, with the actors rolling up and down through their ranges in a way that would make Edith Evans proud" (Freeman 357).
32. I saw this production by the Roundabout Theatre Company of Oscar Wilde's *The Importance of Being Earnest,* directed by Brian Bedford, on January 5, 2011 at the American Airlines Theatre in New York City.
33. Marvin Carlson, *Performance: A Critical Introduction,* 2nd ed. (New York: Routledge, 2004) 5.
34. Ibid.
35. Jean-Paul Sartre, *Being and Nothingness: A Phenomenological Essay on Ontology,* trans. Hazel E. Barnes (New York: Washington Square, 1984) 89.
36. Ibid. 87.
37. Ibid. 89.
38. Ibid.
39. Robert J. Yanal, "Self-Deception and the Experience of Fiction," *Ratio* 20 (2007): 108–121.
40. Sartre 101.
41. Ibid. 102.
42. Ibid. 102–103.
43. Johan Huizinga, *Homo Ludens: A Study of the Play-Element in Culture* (London: Beacon, 1955) 1.
44. Wilde, *Plays* 253.
45. Ibid.

46. Vanhoutte 83.
47. Clifton Snider, "Synchronicity and the Trickster in *The Importance of Being Earnest*," *The Wildean* 27 (2005): 57–58.
48. Jeremy Lalonde, "A 'Revolutionary Outrage': *The Importance of Being Earnest* as Social Criticism," *Modern Drama* 48.4 (Winter 2005): 660.
49. Wilde, *Plays* 271.
50. Ibid. 258.
51. Bertolt Brecht, "A Short Organum for the Theatre," *Brecht on Theatre*, ed. and trans. John Willett (New York: Hill and Wang, 1964) 190.
52. Adolf Barth, "Oscar Wilde's 'Comic Refusal': A Reassessment of *The Importance of Being Earnest*," *Archiv fur das Studium der neueren Sprachen und Literaturen* 216 (1979): 128.
53. Wilde, *Plays* 258.
54. Ibid.
55. Ibid. 259.
56. Joseph S. Catalano, "Successfully Lying to Oneself: A Sartrean Perspective," *Philosophy and Phenomenology Research* 50.4 (January 1990): 676.
57. Ibid. 677.
58. Timothy Chambers, "The elevator effect," *Radical Philosophy* 156 (July/August 2009): 57.
59. Forest Pyle, "Extravagance; Or, Salomé's Kiss," *The Journal of Pre-Raphaelite Studies* 7 (1998): 40.
60. Ibid. 42.
61. Linda Hutcheon and Michael Hutcheon, " 'Here's Looking at You Kid': The Empowering Gaze in *Salome*," *Profession* (1998): 11.
62. Ibid.
63. Pyle 41.
64. Wilde, *Plays* 68.
65. "Stay," *Oxford English Dictionary*, 2nd ed. 1989.
66. Michael Y. Bennett, "Brecht in the Wilde: *Salome*'s Liminal Spaces and the Storyteller," *Journal of Theatre and Drama* 7.8 (2001/2002): 146. For a longer discussion of this, see Bennett 146–147. The idea of Salome being "like" something was, for the essay I am citing here, developed for the purposes of establishing Salome's liminality *in order* to argue that Wilde's *Salome* anticipated some of Brecht's notions of theatre. The current chapter, when discussing *Earnest*, also cites Brecht. However, I am not trying to reestablish the idea of Wilde anticipating Brecht in this essay. Liminality, though not stated quite as directly as in my previous discussion on liminality, is vital to

understanding Wilde's *Salome* and for *Earnest,* as well. If my approach here was to focus more directly on liminality, I could, instead, state the central argument of this essay by asserting that *bunburying (for Algernon, Jack, and Salome) is a liminal state and liminal practice.*
67. Wilde, *Plays* 72.
68. Ibid. 85.
69. Ibid. 91.
70. Ibid.

CHAPTER 2

1. Luigi Pirandello, *Six Characters in Search of an Author,* trans. Edward Storer (Mineola: Dover Publications, Inc., 1998) 1. I have elected to use the earliest English translation (1922) of Pirandello's initial text that premiered in 1921. Since this book aims to capture moments in time, I believe that Pirandello's subsequent editions and alterations of the text bastardized his original intention (making too many concessions for the audience), thus losing the raw response of the 1921 Italian audience.
2. "When the theories of liberal democracy were transplanted, by a purely intellectual process, to a period and to countries whose stage of development and whose practical needs were utterly different from those of Western Europe in the nineteenth century, sterility and disillusionment were the inevitable sequel. Rationalism can create a utopia, but cannot make it real. The liberal democracies scattered throughout the world by the peace settlement of 1919 were the product of abstract theory, stuck no roots in the soil, and quickly shrivelled away."
   (Edward Hallett Carr, *The Twenty Years' Crisis: An Introduction to the Study of International Relations* [New York: Harper & Row, Publishers, 1964] 27)

   Another contributing factor to the failure of international peace, as Carr points out, was the ever-present power factor affecting the League of Nations, despite the formal equality and the participation of all. The founders of the League of Nations "entertained no such illusions" of equality: originally, it was thought that only the Great Powers would constitute the League.
   (Carr 104)

3. R. J. Overy, *The Inter-War Crisis 1919–1939,* 2nd ed. (Harlow, England: Pearson Longman, 2007) 3–4.
4. Ibid. 9.
5. Ibid. 11.
6. Ibid. 38.

7. Overy 19. This social unrest led to a strike wave that swept through Europe: for example, 1,165 strikes involving over 1 million workers in 1918 in Britain and a spate of strikes in Germany in 1917 and 1918 (Overy 19).
8. Overy 23.
9. Ibid. 23.
10. Overy 27–28. Before the war, eastern Europe exported 50 percent of the wheat supplies to western Europe. By 1929, the industrialized western European states got 94 percent of their wheat from the United States (Overy 28).
11. Overy 30.
12. Ibid. 48–49.
13. Ibid. 39.
14. David Cassidy, *Einstein and Our World* (New Jersey: Humanities Press, 1995) 65.
15. Overy 45.
16. Modris Eksteins, *Rites of Spring: The Great War and the Birth of the Modern Age* (New York: Anchor Books, 1989) 211. Eksteins continues on to discuss the interiority of the soldier:

> While most soldiers retained their sense of duty, some began to express themselves about the other aspects of their dichotomous predicament—their feeling of alienation, marginality, and, at the same time, novelty; that is, the idea that the world was in the throes of destruction, which now seemed irreversible, but was also in the process of renewal, which seemed inevitable. In this latter process lay a reality of astounding implications: the soldier represented a creative force. As an agent of both destruction and regeneration, of death and rebirth, the soldier inclined to see himself as a "frontier" personality, as a paladin of change and new life. He was a traveler who had journeyed, on order, to the limits of existence, and there on the periphery he "lived" in a unique way, on the edge of no man's land, on the margin of normal categories.
>
> (211)

Eksteins concludes that "the war entailed a 'journey inward' for soldiers, but a parallel journey was taken by civilians at home. Censorship and propaganda played the major role in this process, blurring, as was their purpose, the reality of the war" (233).
17. Eksteins 210.
18. Overy 7.
19. Ibid. 7.
20. First, Italy had a relatively small population and its late urban growth reflected the lack of many materials needed to industrialize and modernize a nation (R. J. B. Bosworth, *Mussolini's Italy:*

Life under the Dictatorship, 1915–1945 [New York: The Penguin Press, 2006] 38). Second, in 1913, Italy's per capita gross national product was 43 compared with an index that put the United States at 100, Britain at 83, France at 56, and Germany at 54 (Bosworth 39). Third, in 1914, 330 out of every 1,000 Italian recruits were illiterate, compared with 220 for Austro-Hungary, 68 for France, and one for Germany (Bosworth 40). And fourth, starvation and malaria were major concerns in prewar Italy (Bosworth 41–42).
21. Bosworth 47.
22. During the war, the infantry (which took 95 percent of the casualties) was made up mostly of peasants, who were paid only 6 percent of a skilled metalworker's wage. And these soldiers were treated with awful contempt by the higher paid senior officers during the war. In 1919, 63 percent of war orphans were peasant children (Bosworth 70).
23. Bosworth 73.
24. Ibid. 94–95.
25. Ibid. 101–104.
26. Ibid. 106.
27. Ibid. 109–110.
28. Ibid. 118.
29. Ibid. 10.
30. Ibid. 123.
31. Millions of days of work were lost to strikes by agricultural and factory workers (Bosworth 124).
32. H. S. Thayer, *Meaning and Action: A Critical History of Pragmatism* (Indianapolis: The Bobbs-Merrill Company, Inc., 1968) 324.
33. Ibid. 328.
34. Ibid. 329. Papini never fully articulated his conception of practice and the practical. Papini was influenced by F. C. S. Schiller, who, recognizing that F. H. Bradley had problems with articulating the above, defines practice as "*the control of experience,*" and practical as "whatever serves, *directly or indirectly,* to control events." Thayer suggests that this is similar to Papini's sense of *action* (Thayer 330–331).
35. Thayer 329.
36. Ibid. 332.
37. Ibid. 324–325.
38. A. James Gregor, *Mussolini's Intellectuals: Fascist Social and Political Thought* (Princeton: Princeton University Press, 2005) 81–82.
39. Ibid. 83.
40. Ibid. 81–83.
41. Ibid. 83.

42. Ibid. 87.
43. Ibid. 86.
44. Ibid. 88.
45. Gaspare Giudice, *Pirandello: A Biography*, trans. Alastair Hamilton (London: Oxford University Press, 1975) 113.
46. Thayer 324.
47. Giudice 76–78.
48. Seth Baumrin, "No Longer in Search of an Author, a Character Defines Herself: Pirandello's *Six Characters in Search of an Author* and Eugenio Barba's Experimental Performance Methodology," *Modern Drama* 44.2 (2001): 174.
49. Giudice 144.
50. Roger W. Oliver, *Dreams of Passion: The Theater of Luigi Pirandello* (New York: New York University Press, 1979) 52. Anne Paolucci, similarly observes in *Six Characters* the "dissolution of what in everyday life we take to be 'personality' " (*Pirandello's Theater: The Recovery of the Modern Stage for Dramatic Art* [Carbondale: Southern Illinois University Press, 1974] 50).
51. Oliver 57–58.
52. Ibid. 62.
53. Anne Paolucci, "Comedy and Paradox in Pirandello's Plays (An Hegelian Perspective)," *The Plays and Fiction of Luigi Pirandello: Selected Essays* by Anne Paolucci (New York: Griffon House Publications, 2009) 89–90.
54. Paolucci 89.
55. It appears that Pirandello made a common mistake when understanding Hegelian idealism: "Idealism" is a term that had been used sporadically by Leibniz and his followers to refer to a type of philosophy that was opposed to *materialism*. Thus, for example, Leibniz had contrasted *Plato* as an idealist with *Epicurus* as a materialist. The opposition to materialism here, together with the fact that in the English-speaking world the Irish philosopher and clergyman George Berkeley (1685–1753) is often taken as a prototypical idealist, has given rise to the assumption that idealism is necessarily an "immaterialist" doctrine. This assumption, however, is mistaken. The idealism of the Germans was not committed to the type of doctrine found in Berkeley according to which immaterial minds, both infinite (God's) and finite (those of humans), were the ultimately real entities, with *apparently* material things to be understood as reducible to states of such minds—that is, to "ideas" in the sense meant by the British empiricists. ("Georg Wilhelm Friedrich Hegel,"

Stanford Encyclopedia of Philosophy http://plato.stanford.edu/entries/hegel, February 6, 2011.)

Note the line, "The idealism of the Germans was not committed to the type of doctrine found in Berkeley according to which immaterial minds, both infinite (God's) and finite (those of humans), were the ultimately real entities." It appears that Pirandello, rather than reading Hegel correctly, understood "reality" through Berkeley's philosophic lens ("immaterial minds...were the ultimate real entities").

56. Pirandello 3.
57. Ibid. 3.
58. Ibid. 5.
59. Ibid. 4.
60. Ibid. 3.
61. Ibid. 2.
62. Ibid. Actually, earlier, the stage directions give the reader the same information (1).
63. Ibid. 6.
64. This idea of seeing oneself in the play brings us to a fascinating production of *Six Characters* in 1989, reviewed by Frank Rich of *The New York Times*. The director, Anatoly Vasiliev, put the audience in the staging of the production, which was in Russian with simultaneous translation via headphones:

> Like Pirandello's six abandoned fictional figures, who invade a theatrical rehearsal to be brought to completion by actors, the audience watching Mr. Vasiliev's "Six Characters" at Pepsico Summerfare finds itself on a stage in the middle of a rehearsal of a seemingly fatuous play. Mr. Vasiliev's actors sit indiscriminately among the spectators. The house lights are up. And, to make an American audience's disorientation complete, the simultaneous translation piped into our headsets is abruptly shut off. What do the theatergoers do? Their behavior is naturally Pirandellian. At the opening performance on Friday night, some pounded and shook their headsets even after the translator, yet another lost character, appeared on stage to render the occasional line. Two women behind me developed an unstoppable case of the giggles...
> (Frank Rich, "Review: Theater Soviet Director Puts the Audience into 'Six Characters,'" *The New York Times* July 24, 1989: C13)

This move by Vasiliev clearly makes the audience, and certainly this reviewer, focus on the audience: on oneself and on the other audience members. While important, this move is not as significant as Vasiliev's "historical twist":

> When Pirandello's play had its premiere in Italy in 1921, the Russian theater was in the midst of its greatest period of experimentation, a revolution against stage realism parallel to the one championed by "Six Characters." But Pirandello's play did not make it to the Soviet Union during that hospitable decade before Stalin snuffed out avant-garde esthetics in favor of Socialist Realism.
>
> Now, of course, the climate in the Soviet Union is right once more for "Six Characters," and Mr. Vasiliev's staging achieves the mating of experimental Soviet stagecraft and Pirandello that, if history had been different, could have been accomplished in Moscow six decades ago. Certainly this production, like the work of such other liberated contemporary Soviet directors as Yuri Lyubimov, is in the tradition of an adventurous Soviet director of the 1920s like Aleksandr Tairov, who overthrew realism to revel in the naked, unabashed theatricality of the theater.
>
> (Rich C13)

Vasiliev's production, I suspect, brought the contemporary 1989 audience into contact with the audiences of the Soviet 1920s; thus, the 1989 audience's focus on the self triply saw themselves as a person living in the United States in 1989, saw (through the actors) their Soviet counterpart, and saw a glimpse into the mind of a Soviet in the 1920s.

65. Pirandello 12.
66. Anthony Petruzzi, "Hermeneutic Retrieval and the Conflict of Styles in Pirandello's *Sei Personaggi in Cerca D'Autore*," *RSQ: Rhetoric Society Quarterly* 27.3 (Summer 1997): 69.
67. Bert O. States, "The Actor's Presence: Three Phenomenal Modes," *Acting (Re)Considered: A Theoretical and Practical Guide,* ed. Philip B. Zarrilli, 2nd ed. (London: Routledge, 2002) 23.
68. Petruzzi 60.

Chapter 3

1. Samuel Beckett, *En attendant Godot* (Paris: Les Éditions de Minuit, 1952) 87.
2. Samuel Beckett, *Waiting for Godot* (New York: Grove Press, 1954) 40.
3. Tony Judt, *Postwar: A History of Europe Since 1945* (New York: Penguin Books, 2005) 86. Given the enormous scope and narrative quality of Judt's book, I use this book to provide the framework for this historical overview and then reference other scholars to provide more depth and details.

4. First, a lack of a steady food supply was the primary concern of the people of France, as demonstrated in a 1946 opinion poll that reported that "food," "bread," and "meat" were the people's top preoccupations (*Postwar* 86). Western Europeans could no longer get amounts of grains from Eastern Europe that they usually depended upon because Eastern Europe was short on food, as well. A series of failed harvests, from 1945 to 1947, exacerbated the situation. Though food was available for purchase from the United States, American dollars were needed to buy the food. Second, a devastated German economy plagued all of Europe. Prior to the war, Germany, for example, "bought 38 percent of Greece's exports and supplied about one-third of the country's imports" (87). This dependence on the German economy for imports and exports was similar for most of Central and Eastern Europe, including other regions, too, like the Netherlands, Belgium, and the Mediterranean. The loss of the German coal industry, which was central to French steel manufacturers, was another reason that a stalled German economy devastated the rest of Europe. And third, there was a lack of American dollars to buy needed goods from the United States. Since much of Europe could not produce goods themselves, in part because of the two above reasons, their reliance on American goods was even stronger. However, without the ability to produce goods to export to the rest of the world, Europe was short on American dollars to buy, not only food, but raw materials and machinery.
5. Judt 89.
6. Ibid. 89
7. "These goods, when sold in each country, would generate so-called 'counterpart funds' in the local currency which could be used according to bilateral agreements reached between Washington and each national government. Some countries used these funds to purchase more imports; others, like Italy, transferred them into their national reserves in anticipation of future foreign exchange needs" (Judt 93).
8. Judt 94. Not speaking specifically about banking, Alan S. Milward observes that "Integration, as evolved between 1947 and 1951, was a formalization of interdependence significantly different in form and final implications from anything previously seen" (Alan S. Milward, *The Reconstruction of Western Europe: 1945–1951* [Berkeley: University of California Press, 1984] 494).
9. Judt 325. The new, now younger, Europe—as postwar births in Europe were significantly up, such as in France where 869,000 babies were born in 1949 compared with 612,000 in 1939—was ready, and in need, of greater consumer consumption. Washing machines,

fridges, toys, clothes were being made in larger and larger quantities while the high demand for these items brought prices down. But, as Judt suggests, "The greatest single measure of European prosperity was the revolution wrought by the family car" (331), where in France, "car ownership rose from less than two million to nearly six million vehicles in the course of the 1950s" (339). In 1951, for example, there were 606,000 new vehicle registrations; that number jumped 30 percent over the next two years, as well (Milward 491).

Much of the reason that the automobile flourished had directly to do with the Marshall Plan. Due to 200 productivity loans of 3 billion francs from the Marshall Plan labor-management "missions," the automobile sector (one of the few recipients of these loans) was able to manufacture cars for mass markets (Kristin Ross, *Fast Cars, Clean Bodies: Decolonization and the Reordering of French Culture* [Cambridge: The MIT Press, 1996] 24). Ross observes the newfound obsession with cars and their connection to the booming economy in *Fast Cars, Clean Bodies: Decolonization and the Reordering of French Culture*:

> Postwar French economic growth was a direct result of having modernized sectors of production that were seen to be vital—and the most vital of these was automobile production. In turn, the augmentation in French buying power after 1949 was used principally to buy cars.
> (19)

> Because, in large part, of the removal of impediments to international commerce, the result of this economic furor was directly seen in steadily growing rates of per capita GDP and GNP. Though even higher in other countries like West Germany and Italy, France per capita national output grew 3.5 percent yearly over the course of the 1950s (compared to 0.7 percent yearly growth from 1913–1950).

(Judt 325)

10. Herbert R. Lottmann relays the events of a supposed meeting between Sartre and Camus that says so much about them and what was going on at that time: "After the beginning of the Korean War, Camus and Sartre sat in the Brasserie Balzar alongside the Sorbonne, arguing their respective positions with some heat. 'Have you thought about what will happen to you when the Russians arrive?' Camus is supposed to have asked Sartre, adding 'Don't stay!' For his part, Camus said that he would join the resistance; Sartre replied that he could never raise a hand against the proletariat. The intensity of Camus' plea, 'If you stay, they'll take not only your life but your honor,' affected Simone de Beauvoir, she confesses in her journal.

In the days following that café meeting, she repeated Camus's argument in her discussions with Sartre. Merleau-Ponty's wife told Sartre, 'What is expected of you is suicide.' Another time, according to Beauvoir, Roger Stéphane pleaded, 'In any case, Sartre, promise me that you'll never confess!'" (Herbert R. Lottmann, *The Left Bank: Writers, Artists, and Politics from the Popular Front to the Cold War* [Boston: Houghton Mifflin Company, 1982] 265–266).

11. Judt 282.
12. Judt 284. However, French political concerns were not just focused on their colonies. France was concerned with positioning itself well within Europe. Stemming originally from the Brussels Conference of December 1950 and from a 1951 French proposal to create a European army (which would simultaneously, "restrict German influence while appeasing American demands for the enrollment of German troops in western defense" [Hitchcock 153]), the European Defense Community (EDC) Treaty was signed on May 27, 1952. Needing parliamentary ratification from the signing nations, the formation of the EDC became a national issue for politicians and the press. The left-leaning presses—*Combat* (Camus' old newspaper), *l'Express,* and *France-Observer*—opposed European rearmament and confrontation with the Soviets, while the center-left *Le Monde* worried that the EDC would strengthen Germany and possibly pull France into liberating Eastern Germany (Hitchcock 172). (France's parliament eventually rejected ratification of the EDC in 1954.)
13. Judt 286.
14. Ross 22.
15. Ross 76. As such, a 1951 investigation/survey in the relatively new *Elle* magazine, entitled "La Francaise, est-elle propre?" ("Is the French Woman Clean?"), caused quite an uproar. Ross draws out the subtle implications of this article:

> "Perhaps certain people (Germans) had left a polluting stain on France, perhaps certain French (collaborators) had to be purged and eliminated, perhaps certain French women (brothel owners and prostitutes) were tainted, perhaps literary language was hopelessly metaphorical and in need of a good scrubbing, but to question the personal hygiene of *la Francaise*—the French woman?... This—as Frantz Fanon said around the same time a propos of France own campaign to colonize Algeria according to the well-known formula 'Let's win over the women and the rest will follow'—is to target the innermost structure of the society itself."
>
> (76–77)

16. Ross 78.

17. There were still significant hurdles to overcome in France: the work of reconstruction was not finished; the populace was now working 52 hours a week (up from 45); Marshall aid was used up; there were coal and steel shortages; and France had a $500–$600 million dollar gap by the end of 1952. Though real earnings were coming back, in France, like in Germany and Italy where there were inflationary pressures and political fragmentation, the standards of living were still quite low due to poor diets, inflation, the maldistribution of income, inequitable taxation, and lower social expenditures. A political fallout—with the Communists capturing 26 percent of the May 1951 vote in France—possibly resulted from this economic fallout, as both Michael J. Hogan and Dirk Stikker suggest.
18. Tony Judt suggests that French intellectuals, in particular, did not know how to deal with the outburst of repression in Central and Eastern Europe from 1947–1954. Many French intellectuals personally had connections to those on trial and, that fact, combined with the fact that totalitarianism was spreading so close to Western Europe meant that what was happening in the Soviet bloc was a prominent matter in France (*Past Imperfect: French Intellectuals, 1944–1954* [Berkeley: University of California Press, 1992] 103–115).
19. Judt 213.
20. Lottmann writes,

> "The Last years of Stalin, years of arbitrary accusations and arrests, placed increased strains on Communist credibility. French Party members and fellow travelers were required to accept not only the purges of veteran Communists once praised for their courage and loyalty, but to write and to make speeches justifying the purges, to visit the countries where they were taking place, just as French collaborationists had been brought to Germany during the war."
>
> (269–270)

21. Judt 210.
22. Ibid. 211.
23. Charles Forsdick labels the debate "the great quarrel" and writes a detailed but compact account of it: Charles Forsdick, "Camus and Sartre: The Great Quarrel," *The Cambridge Companion to Camus*, ed. Edward J. Hughes (Cambridge: Cambridge University Press, 2007) 118–130.
24. It should also be noted that 1952 France saw the publication of Frantz Fanon's *Black Skin White Masks (Peau noire, masques blancs)*, which, as Michael Kelly argues, was one of the most influential applications of the framework for analyzing prejudice that Sartre provided in his

1946 work, *Portrait of the Anti-Semite (Réflexions sur la question juive)* (Michael Kelly, *The Cultural and Intellectual Rebuilding of France after the Second World War* [Houndsmills: Palgrave Macmillan, 2004] 161–162).
25. Though existentialism had the popular appeal and the intellectual dominance in France, Kelly argues that existentialism was contested from the very beginning, most especially from the Catholic right-wing movements (176).
26. David Drake, *Intellectuals and Politics in Post-War France* (London: Palgrave, 2002) 3–4.
27. For an in-depth account of Sartre and *Les Temps modernes,* see, Anna Boschetti, *The Intellectual Enterprise: Sartre and Les Temps Modernes,* trans. Richard C. McCleary (Evanston: Northwestern University Press, 1988).
28. Drake 24.
29. Drake 23. Drake notes that the PCF was not the only group of Marxists: many members of the Socialist SFIO thought of themselves as Marxists (24). Annie Cohen-Solal describes the events that led Sartre to fully support the PCF. (This happens to be right around the time of Sartre and Camus' public quarrel in *Les Temps modernes.*) Sartre, at the time in Rome, heard about the May 28, 1952, demonstration by 20,000 to 30,000 supporters of the PCF in the streets of Paris protesting the arrival of American general Matthew Ridgeway, who represented MaCarthy's witch hunt against Communists. What truly upset Sartre was the arrest of Jacques Duclos, the secretary of the PCF, for carrying pigeons in a car, which was argued by the Pinay government as a sign of carrier pigeons for a Communist plot against the state (the pigeons were a gift and Duclos was going home with his wife to cook them for dinner and for that, Duclos spent one month in jail). Sartre hastily returned to Paris and began writing "The Communist and Peace," which signaled his rapprochement with the Communists, and was published (the first part, that is) in *Les Temps modernes* in July 1952. See, Annie Cohen-Solal, *Sartre: A Life,* trans. Anna Cancogni, ed. Norman Macafee (New York: Pantheon Books, 1987) 327–331.
30. Drake 27.
31. Ibid. 30.
32. Lottmann notes the danger of Camus' approach to the Communists: "Socialists had to choose between the Communist doctrine that ends justify means—i.e., that murder can be a legitimate act—and the rejection of Marxism except as a critical tool ... In refusing to choose between Communism and capitalism, in trying to 'save

bodies,' Camus became (or so charged Emmanuel d'Astier de la Vigerie) an unwitting accomplice of capitalism" (260–261).
33. Drake 84. Germaine Brée offers a different point of view of the quarrel and the significance of *The Rebel*: "Although the controversies that fused around The Rebel reveal much concerning the politico-literary tangles of the time, they missed the fact that Camus had intuitively glimpsed the French political situation returning to relative normalcy... A new situation was emerging which did not fit the catastrophist patterns of social change through a proletarian revolution" (Germaine Brée, *Camus and Sartre: Crisis and Commitment* [New York: Delacorte Press, 1972] 6–7).
34. Ibid. 82.
35. For possibly the most concise and understandable overview of the works of Sartre and Camus, as this book covers all of the major texts of each philosopher in chronological order in simple jargon-free language, see Leo Pollmann, *Sartre and Camus: Literature of Existence,* trans. Helen and Gregor Sebba (New York: Frederik Ungar Publishing Co., 1970). For another excellent book that examines the difference between the two philosophers—this one goes deeper into the philosophical implications of each philosophy—see, Peter Royle, *The Sartre-Camus Controversy: A Literary and Philosophical Critique* (Ottawa: University of Ottawa Press, 1982). For more on Camus' philosophy, see the very readable, *The Cambridge Companion to Camus,* ed. Edward J. Hughes (Camridge: Cambridge University Press, 2007). For more on Sartre's philosophy, see the sometimes unreadable but extremely complex and in-depth, *The Cambridge Companion to Sartre,* ed. Christina Howells (Cambridge: Cambridge University Press, 1992).
36. Royle describes the two philosophers' sense of the absurd: "Whereas for Camus the absurd is the relation between man and the universe for Sartre, insofar as on can properly use the term at all, it is absolute Being itself that is absurd; or perhaps we should say that for him the absurd is a relation between two relations, the subjective and objective relations of man to the world; which is another way of saying that we invent meanings instead of discovering them" (48).
37. Albert Camus, *The Rebel: An Essay on Man in Revolt* (New York: Vintage Books, 1956) 15.
38. Camus 6.
39. Royle 49.
40. Jean-Paul Sartre, "Existentialism is a Humanism," *Existentialism: From Dostoevsky to Sartre,* ed. Walter Kaufman (New York: Plume Book, 1975) 349.

41. Camus 11.
42. Ibid. 22.
43. Ibid.
44. Pollmann 116.
45. Ronald Aronson, *Camus and Sartre: The Story of a Friendship and the Quarrel That Ended It* (Chicago: The University of Chicago Press, 2004) 115. Whereas Camus was fiercely against Stalinism, Judt explains how Sartre and others like him responded to Stalin: "Unable to join the Communists and unwilling to part company from them, a significant number of prominent French Intellectuals devoted themselves not to condemning or defending the works of Stalin but to explaining them" (*Past Imperfect* 119).
46. Francis Jeanson, "Albert Camus, of The Soul in Revolt," *Sartre and Camus: A Historic Confrontation,* ed. and trans. David A. Sprintzen and Adrian van der Hoven (Amherst, New York: Humanity Books, 2004) 95–96.
47. Jeanson 101.
48. Albert Camus, "A Letter to the Editor of *Les Temps modernes,*" *Sartre and Camus: A Historic Confrontation,* ed. and trans. David A. Sprintzen and Adrian van der Hoven (Amherst, New York: Humanity Books, 2004) 111–112.
49. Jean-Paul Sartre, "Reply to Albert Camus," *Sartre and Camus: A Historic Confrontation,* ed. and trans. David A. Sprintzen and Adrian van der Hoven (Amherst, New York: Humanity Books, 2004) 155.
50. Sartre 155.
51. Ibid. 158.
52. Ibid.
53. Aronson 2.
54. Actually, Beckett published *En attendant Godot* in Paris in 1952. The English version, *Waiting for Godot,* which he translated himself, was not published until 1954 by Grove Press. Whether or not this is the *same* text is a matter for translation theorists to debate. I am going to be using the English text not only because I am a native English speaker and my audience is English-speaking academics, but the fact that it was published after the 1952 quarrel between Sartre and Camus means that it is possible that some of these ideas that were swirling around in their debate may have been unconsciously inserted or highlighted in Beckett's translation choices (especially the grammar associated with the verbs "be" and "do"). See especially my discussion in this chapter of Beckett's translation of "Tu crois?" to "Am I?"
55. Milward 490.

56. Ibid. 491.
57. See "Chapter 1" in, Michael Y. Bennett, *Reassessing the Theatre of the Absurd: Camus, Beckett, Ionesco, Genet, and Pinter* (New York: Palgrave Macmillan, 2011) 27–51. Elsewhere, I argue that in *Waiting for Godot*, "essence precedes experience and, thus, Beckett's thought is a version of Cartesian Rationalism, not existentialism" (Michael Y. Bennett, " 'The Essential Doesn't Change': Essence Precedes Experience and Cartesian Rationalism in Samuel Beckett's *Waiting for Godot*," *Notes on Contemporary Literature* 42.1 (January 2012): 6). I suggest in my analysis of *Waiting for Godot* that Beckett is, as Peter Royle calls Albert Camus, a "disabused heir of the Enlightenment" (Ibid.).
58. Vreneli Farber, "Review of *Waiting for Godot*," *Theatre Journal* 53.4 (December 2001): 653.
59. Michael Y. Bennett, "Review of *Waiting for Godot*," *Theatre Journal* 62.1 (March 2010): 110.
60. Ibid.
61. Holland Cotter, "A Broken City. A Tree. Evening," *The New York Times* December 2, 2007: 2:1.
62. Ibid.
63. When talking about the set for *Waiting for Godot* and how it reflects the feelings of the actors being "trapped," Michèle Lester writes that "Beckett uses the staging of the three basic elements of theatre... to draw the audience in, but often he employs precisely the same elements to keep them out" ("Through the Looking Glass: Beckett," *Anamnesia: Private and Public Memory in Modern French Culture* [Bern: Peter Lang, 2009] 196). I drew upon a visual to represent this, but it is more than that, for it depends on how the audience perceives it. Mary Bryden claims that "Beckett's scenes are not a 'setting' but is simply a space in which movement and/or stillness can occur" ("Deleuze Reading Beckett," *Beckett and Philosophy*, ed. Richard Lane [New York: Palgrave, 2002] 87).
64. Much of Camus' *The Rebel* focuses on the master-slave relationship. One should also note here the ever-present influence of Hegel's study of the master-slave dialectic in his *Phenomenology of Spirit*. Though Hegel is beyond the scope of the present study, it should be stated here that Camus was very conscious of Hegel's master-slave dialectic. (Camus deals specifically with Hegel's master-slave dialectic in his chapter, "The Decides," in *The Rebel* [133–148].) By extension, given Beckett's broad understanding of philosophy, it is easy to conceive that Beckett, as well, was probably very aware of Hegel's master-slave dialectic.

65. Thomas Cousineau comments on this dichotomy by writing that "Beckett's work seems in general to invite interpretation from two related perspectives. On the one hand, we have the conflict of mind and body, between the inner psychic world and the outer world of material phenomena, and, on the other, the opposition between the real self and its alienated simulacra" (Thomas Cousineau, "Descartes, Lacan, and *Murphy*," *College Literature* 11.3 (1984): 231).

   On the other hand, Ulrika Maude believes that "It is now widely concurred that the Beckettian characters' experience of the world is a markedly physical, bodily experience," seeming to imply that it is the body, more than the mind, that we are to experience and that "It seems to be the body... that gives the characters assurance of their existence" ("The Body of Memory: Beckett and Merleau-Ponty," *Beckett and Philosophy*, ed. Richard Lane [New York: Palgrave, 2002] 108).
66. Jude Meche has also noticed Beckett's specific use of language, stating that "Beckett painstakingly traces the relationship between language and identity in any number of his works" ("Beckett's *Not I:* Empty Speech and Obsession in Mouth's Dialogue," *Studies in the Humanities* 25.1–2 (1998): 109).
67. This paragraph and the following three paragraphs are adapted for this chapter: see Bennett, *Reassessing the Theatre of the Absurd* 39–41.
68. "Temperament," *Oxford English Dictionary*, 2nd ed., 1989.
69. "Disposition," *Oxford English Dictionary*, 2nd ed., 1989.
70. "Character," *Oxford English Dictionary*, 2nd ed., 1989.
71. Camus *Rebel* 11.
72. Pollman pithily sums up the idea of change, choice, and being: "I decide, my actions decide, what man is" (8).
73. Pollmann describes the centrality of change and being in Sartre's philosophy this way:

    > For man is essentially choice, a constantly redrawn preliminary sketch for something else, both in knowing and in acting, and this posits the annihilation or, to put it more understandably, the bracketing out and subjective nullification of everything that is not known and not chosen... Thus, man is neither the one nor the other, neither thing nor nothingness. Neither can be defined, say, as flux, for flux is predictable, whereas man is at every moment new, free choice.
    >
    > (7–8)

74. Thomas Cousineau suggests, "Beckett's fiction resembles contemporary philosophy in its determination to unmask illusions, yet neither the fiction nor the philosophy can pretend to say what lies beyond" ("Watt: Language as Interdiction and Consolation," *The Beckett*

Studies Reader, ed. S. E. Gontarski [Gainsville: University Press of Florida, 1993] 74).

75. I am noting here that both characters, particularly Vladimir, are posed with a philosophically disconcerting situation. Angela Moorjani seems to capture the tone Beckett creates here:

> ... the role of seeing as structuring and positioning device in the tortured relationship between self and other (within and without the subject) in Beckett's writing. Rendering an injured object visible to the eyes is an intriguing approach to Beckett's ever renewed attempts at failing to find a visible form for the inner chaos. As we have seen, reversible perspective is one of his ways of questioning the stability of vision: figure and ground, inside and outside, contained and container, image and frame oscillate in and out of focus..."
> ("Beckett and Psychoanalysis," *Palgrave Advances in Samuel Beckett Studies*, ed. Lois Oppenheim [New York: Palgrave Macmillan, 2004] 179–180)

76. "Ooze," *Oxford English Dictionary*, 2nd ed., 1989.
77. Andrew Gibson has come to a similar conclusion that in the end, Beckett is more concerned with the journey than the answers: "The extraordinary implication... is that Beckett's art is neither a representation, nor an expression, nor an indication of truth. It is rather a disposition, a way of waiting for a truth, of clearing the ground for it, even conjuring its arrival" ("Beckett and Badiou," *Beckett and Philosophy*, ed. Richard Lane [New York: Palgrave, 2002] 102).
78. For a more decidedly nonexistential view of Godot and how potential nothingness exists in the play, see: Michael Y. Bennett, "Sartre's 'The Wall' and Beckett's *Waiting for Godot*: Existential and Non-Existential Nothingness," *Notes on Contemporary Literature* 39.5 (November 2009): 2–3.
79. Meche says, "Many of Beckett's critics incorporate Jacques Lacan's theories on psychology and language into their considerations of his work" (102). This oozing of the tree is similar to the idea Thomas Cousineau elaborates on in his article "Descartes, Lacan, and *Murphy*." Cousineau writes that "per both Beckett and Lacan a central concern is the process through which the primordial subject moves out of its original undifferentiated experience into the world of customs, cultural norms, and socially sanctioned rationality" (225). In other words, Beckett, like Lacan, was interested in how one can go from being innately themselves, to who they become when they come in contact with the rest of the world. In essence, a person is who they were, and who they are after being influenced by all these things. In some way, it can be seen "that every self image is based upon a misconception" (Lester 194).

One is not just the tree, nor just the pus, but the tree and the pus, like a child seeing and understanding his image in the mirror for the first time, aware that they are at once the same and yet separate:

> The infant is drawn out of the real and into the imaginary by the mirror phase, where he encounters his image, partly that image which he himself sees in the mirror, but partly as well the image conveyed to him by the eyes of others. Prior to this phase, the body is experienced as an undifferentiated chaos. Only through the adoption of the unified, bounded image offered by the mirror, does the discovery of the self as a potential unity arise.
> (Cousineau "Descartes, Lacan, and Murphy" 225–226)

CHAPTER 4

1. Edward Albee, *Who's Afraid of Virginia Woolf?* (New York: Signet, 1983) 241–242.
2. Martin Esslin, *The Theatre of the Absurd* (Garden City: Anchor Books, 1961) xxi.
3. Jeane Luere, "*Terror and Violence in Edward Albee?: From Who's Afraid of Virginia Woolf? to Marriage Play*," *South Central Review* 7.1 (Spring 1990): 51.
4. In a nice twist on a belabored theme, Dan Ducker suggests that this play is not just about the failure of communication, but also its *success*: in one scene that Ducker quotes, "George reacts to a failure of communication [with Nick] as a threat to civilization," seeing that communication is the cement that holds together civilization" (" 'Pow!' 'Snap!' 'Pouf!' ": The Modes of Communication in *Who's Afraid of Virginia Woolf?*" *CLA Journal* 26.4 (June 1983): 465–466.)
5. Jill R. Deans, "Albee's Substitute Children: Reading Adoption as a Performance," *Journal of Dramatic Theory and Criticism* 13.2 (Spring 1999): 57.
6. I am not the first one to dwell specifically on fear (though I take it up in much greater detail). See Matthew Roudané, "*Who's Afraid of Virginia Woolf?*: Toward the Marrow," *The Cambridge Companion to Edward Albee,* ed. Stephen Bottoms (Cambridge: Cambridge University Press, 2005) 54–55.
7. Ibid.
8. Tony Judt, *Postwar: A History of Europe Since 1945* (New York: Penguin Books, 2005) 210.
9. See Joy Flasch, "Games People Play in *Who's Afraid of Virginia Woolf?*" *Modern Drama* 10 (1967): 280–288; Louis Paul, "A Game Analysis of Albee's *Who's Afraid of Virginia Woolf?*: The Core of Grief,"

Literature and Psychology 17 (1967): 47–51; C. Warren Robertson, "An Analysis of *Who's Afraid of Virginia Woolf?*" *Publications of the Mississippi Philological Association* (1986): 112–120; Claire Virginia Eby, "Fun and Games with George and Nick: Competitive Masculinity in *Who's Afraid of Virginia Woolf?*" *Modern Drama* 50.4 (Winter 2007): 601–618.

10. Stephen J. Bottoms, *Albee: Who's Afraid of Virginia Woolf?* (Cambridge: Cambridge University Press, 2000) 5.
11. Ibid. 5–7.
12. Albee 180.
13. Ibid. 67.
14. James T. Patterson, *Grand Expectations: The United States, 1945–1974* (New York: Oxford University Press, 1996) 407–408. Much like Tony Judt's *Postwar* that framed the history section of Chapter 3, given *Grand Expectations'* similar scope and authority, I will be using Patterson's book to frame the history in this chapter.
15. Ibid. 410.
16. Ibid. 418. The fear of placing nuclear warheads atop missiles like Sputnik was legitimate, especially since the United States had difficulty predicting the behavior of Khrushchev (John Lewis Gaddis, *The Cold War: A New History* [New York: Penguin Books, 2005] 68). Khrushchev stood in stark contrast to Eisenhower: The supremely self-confident Eisenhower was always in command of himself, his administration, and certainly the military forces of the United States. Khrushchev, in contrast, was excess personified: he could be boisterously clownish, belligerently cloying, aggressively insecure (Gaddis 69).
17. Patterson 487–488.
18. Howard Jones, *The Bay of Pigs* (Oxford: Oxford University Press, 2008) 3. "The United States in April 1961 embarked on a new and more aggressive Cold War policy that did not become evident until a congressional investigation published its findings fifteen years later" (Jones 4).
19. Jones suggests that the Bay of Pigs was the result of "a nearly personal conflict": Powerful egos confronted each other from across the Caribbean, and one suspects that by April 1961 Kennedy had been drawn into a nearly personal conflict with a rival state leader who had masterfully goaded him into irrational actions that played themselves out at the Bay of Pigs and left an enduring legacy (7).
20. Patterson 498. All in the attempt to eliminate Castro, in fall 1961, the Kennedy administration created a top-secret program run by Robert Kennedy (code-named Operation Mongoose) and, before

linking it to a revived CIA-Mafia assassination effort, completed the preparation of Project ZR/RIFLE (Jones 154).
21. Ibid. 498. Gaddis recounts an encounter by Kennedy and Khrushchev that paints a slightly different portrait than Patterson's: John F. Kennedy, for example, found the Soviet leader's ideological self-confidence thoroughly intimidating when he encountered Khrushchev at the 1961 Vienna summit: "He just beat hell out of me," the new president admitted. Kennedy had "seemed rather stunned," British prime minister Harold Macmillan noted shortly thereafter, "like somebody meeting Napoleon (at the height of his power) for the first time" (Gaddis 84).
22. Ibid. 498–499.
23. Ibid. 502.
24. Gaddis 80. The fall of 1962 was the peak and end, one can say, of the true nuclear crisis: Nuclear alarms—even alerts—occurred after 1962, but there were no more nuclear crises of the kind that had dominated the superpower relationship since the late 1940s. Instead a series of Soviet-American agreements began to emerge, at first tacit, later explicit, acknowledging the danger nuclear weapons posed to the capitalist and communist worlds alike (Gaddis 81).
25. "Kennedy himself remained personally very popular throughout his presidency. Along with the booming economy, which after 1962 seemed capable of almost anything, the magnified mystique of the presidency stimulated ever-greater expectations among liberals and others who imagined that government possessed big answers to big problems. The revolution of popular expectations, a central dynamic of the 1960s, owed a good deal of its strength to the glorification of presidential activism that Kennedy successfully sought to foment" (Patterson 461).
26. Ibid. 450–451. For a tremendously in-depth examination of American economics during that general period, see Michael French, *US Economic History Since 1945* (Manchester: Manchester University Press, 1997).
27. Patterson 451.
28. Ibid. 451.
29. Ibid. 452.
30. Ibid. 443–444.
31. Ibid. 444.
32. 1960 saw the birth of the "sit-in" when four African American freshmen at North Carolina A&T College in Greensboro, NC, sat at the counter to be served at the local Woolworth department store until the store closed half an hour early (Paterson 430). The sit-in

movement grew and it was fueled by unsung local activists, many of whom came to be leaders in the Civil Rights movement years later (Paterson 431). For Mary L. Dudziak, the Cold War and the Civil Rights movement were closely intertwined. The diplomatic impact of race during the Cold War was notable given that the United States had to ensure that democracy was appealing to other peoples and nations. Mary L. Dudziak, *Cold War Civil Rights: Race and the Image of American Democracy* (Princeton: Princeton University Press, 2000) 6. With a similar argument but different details, Thomas Borstelmann writes a sweeping history about race relations and the Cold War. See Thomas Borstelmann, *The Cold War and the Color Line: American Race Relations in the Global Arena* (Cambridge: Harvard University Press, 2001) 85–171.

Coming out of the era of "McCarthyism," Civil Rights groups had to carefully balance, "making it clear that their reform efforts were meant to fill out the contours of American democracy, and not to challenge or undermine it," so as not to be thought of as "subversive" like others who criticized American society; thus, there was no room for a broad critique of racial oppression within the strictures of Cold War politics (Dudziak 11). Despite the obstacles to the expansion of the Civil Rights movement, the United States needed reform "in order to make credible the government's argument about race and democracy" (Dudziak 14).

33. However, this statement is not entirely true, as Gottlob Frege (1848–1925) and his philosophical work on logic and mathematics were not a response to logical positivism, yet influenced Russell and Wittgenstein.

34. Frege similarly thought that while ordinary language could express emotions and certain nuanced meanings, ordinary language could not work for a system of demonstrative science. Whereas Russell and Whitehead saw logic as a perfected version of ordinary language, Frege saw the two as incompatible (Avrum Stroll, *Twentieth-Century Analytic Philosophy* [New York: Columbia University Press, 2000] 12). There are very few histories of analytic philosophy, despite its centrality to twentieth-century philosophy. Stroll's book is the most straightforward. Frederick Copelston wades into the fray, but his book on the matter is not a part of his nine-volume *A History of Philosophy*, and therefore is not really a history (but is more of a discussion), and he only goes up to Wittgenstein's *Philosophical Investigations* (Frederick Copelston, *Contemporary Philosophy: Studies of Logical Positivism and Existentialism* [London: Continuum, 1972]). The third book that serves as some sort of history of analytic

philosophy is a two-volume behemoth: Scott Soames, *Philosophical Analysis in the Twentieth Century: Volume 1: The Dawn of Analysis* (Princeton: Princeton University Press, 2003); Scott Soames, *Philosophical Analysis in the Twentieth Century: Volume 2: The Age of Meaning* (Princeton: Princeton University Press, 2003). While this two-volume work is the most in-depth of the books by the three scholars discussed, and therefore I would highly recommend it as the place to go for more information on the subject, the tremendous depth of philosophical discussion is entirely unnecessary for this chapter. At the risk of appearing to lack academic rigor and vigor, I am only referencing Stroll's history of analytic philosophy for two reasons: (1) the depth of Stroll's book is appropriate for the scholarly conversation that I am undertaking here, and (2) Stroll develops a true historical *narrative,* which fits much better with the scope and purpose of this book and the other chapters.

35. Stroll 11. For full account of this dispute, as told through the dispute of two men, Russell and Bradley, see Stewart Candlish, *The Russell/Bradley Dispute and Its Significance for Twentieth-Century Philosophy* (New York: Palgrave Macmillan, 2009). Russell's logical atomism was a response to the idealism of his contemporary Hegelians, F. H, Bradley and McTaggart. As a monistic philosophy, idealism suggested that reality is a sum of its parts, a totality, where the parts are necessarily related to each other and cannot be separated without distortion. Therefore, no single statement is either ever totally true or totally false (i.e., they are at most partially true or partially false). Russell's response to this assertion was that reality was composed of discrete facts made of particular things (Stroll 33):

> Russell emphasizes that both facts and particulars belong to the external objective world and are to be distinguished from the beliefs and linguistic units that allow us to think and talk about them. Propositions describe facts and names denote particulars ... a fact itself is neither true nor false ... What are true or false are propositions (or perhaps beliefs) about facts.
>
> (Stroll 37)

Russell simply says, "You cannot name a fact ... The only thing you can do is to assert it ... " (Ibid. 38). Logical atomism is metaphysical in that mathematical logic, as it is argued, mirrors the structure of reality (Ibid. 43). In short, Russell's "scientific philosophy" was an empiricist epistemology (Ibid. 45), as Russell argues that "The fundamental epistemological principle in the analysis of propositions containing descriptions is this: Every proposition which we can understand must be composed holly of constituents with which we are acquainted" (Stroll 51). As a theorist of perception, Russell had three possible responses to understanding the external world: direct realism, representative realism, and phenomenalism. Direct realism suggests that sometimes humans "see" the world/an object just like it really is. Representative realism argues that humans *infer* the true nature of the object from the *image,* not the object itself, but how we "see" the image (i.e., how light reflects to our eyes and all the way to our brains). Phenomenalism suggests that when we "see" an object, we are only aware of various sensations: that external objects just happen to be identical to the sense experiences (that we either have or may have). Russell rejected direct realism and went back and forth between representative realism and phenomenalism (Stroll 49–50).

36. Beginning in 1924, a group of intellectuals (mostly scientists and mathematicians) met weekly in Vienna to discuss three main topics: Einstein's special and general theories of relativity, Schlick's 1918 book, *General Theory of Knowledge,* and Wittgenstein's *Tractatus.* Naming their group the "Vienna Circle" (Der Wiener Kreis), these intellectuals developed logical positivism, an outgrowth of a narrow reading of *Tractatus.* For a full explanation as to why the Vienna Circle's reading of Wittgenstein's *Tractatus* was a narrow one, see Stroll 56–64. Their interpretation was that philosophy was a second-order discipline, which using logic as an ideal language, allowed them to describe and articulate the principles and concepts of science, in their opinion, the first-order discipline (Stroll 54).

37. Rudolph Carnap joined the group in 1926 and became the unofficial spokesperson for logical positivism, while A. J. Ayer's *Language, Truth, and Logic* brought logical positivism international fame (Ibid. 55). However, because of the political turbulence of the 1930s, and the fact that many of the Vienna Circle were Jewish, its philosophers and its theories moved to England and, especially, the United States. By 1940, some of logical positivism's most distinguished thinkers, Phillipp Frank, Carnap, and Feigl, taught permanently in the United States (Ibid. 56).

38. Ibid. 64.
39. Ibid. 65–66.
40. Ibid. 68.
41. Stroll 70. Quine's 1950 seminal article "Two Dogmas of Empiricism" rejected the analytic-synthetic division and the reductive thesis of logical positivism, arguing for an empiricism without these two dogmas that he called "naturalized epistemology" (Stroll 70–71). Quine and

his close friend, Carnap, debated the status of these two principles for the rest of their lives (Stroll 71).
42. Ibid. 84–86.
43. Ibid. 125.
44. Ibid. 126.
45. "What is time? Who can easily and briefly explain this? Who can comprehend this even in thought, so as to express it in a word? Yet what do we discuss more familiarly and knowingly in conversation than time? Surely we understand it when we talk about it, and also understand it when we hear others talk about it. What, then, is time? If no one asks me, I know; if I want to explain it to someone who does ask me, I do not know" (Augustine *Confessions* qtd. in Stroll 127).
46. Stroll 126–130.
47. Ibid. 126.
48. Ibid. 130.
49. Ibid. 132–133. The following is a "case" (§19 and §20) followed by a "language-game" (§21) (Ludwig Wittgenstein, *Philosophical Investigations: The English Text of the Third Edition*, Trans. G. E. M. Anscombe [New York: Macmillan Publishing Co., Inc., 1958] 8–10):

> 19. ... is the call "Slab!" in example (2) a sentence or a word? ... But why should I not on the contrary have called the sentence "Bring me a slab" a *lengthening* of the sentence "Slab!"?—Because if you shout "Slab!" you really mean: "Bring me a slab."—But how do you do this: how do you *mean that* while you *say* "Slab!"? Do you say the unshortened sentence to yourself? And why should I translate the call "Slab!" into a different expression in order to say what someone means by it? And if they mean the same thing—why should I not say: "When he says 'Slab!' he means 'Slab!' "? ... But when I call "Slab!" then what I want is, *that he should bring me a slab!*—Certainly, but does "wanting this" consist in thinking in some form or other a different sentence from the one you utter?—
>
> ...
>
> 21. Imagine a language-game in which A asks and B reports the number of slabs or blocks in a pile, or the colours and shapes of the building-stones that are stacked in such-and-such a place—Such a report might run: "Five slabs." Now what is the difference between the report or statement "Five slabs" and the order "Five slabs!"?—Well, it is the part which uttering these words plays in the language-game. No doubt the tone of voice and the look with which they are uttered, and much else besides, will also be different. But we could also imagine the tone's being the same—for an order and a

report can be spoken in a *variety* of tones of voice and with various expressions of face—the difference being only in the application ....

50. Austin argues for three different types of speech acts: phonetic (the act of uttering a noise); phatic (the act of uttering vocables or words that belong to a grammar or vocabulary); and rhetic (the performance of the act of uttering vocables and words that have sense and reference (Stroll 173). In addition, Austin delineates three types of "forces": locutionary (speaking about the utterance's meaning); illocutionary (speaking about an utterance using words in their standard sense to say what one should do); and perlocutionary (the result of an illocutionary force in that one is persuaded to do something) (Stroll 173–174).
51. Stroll 174.
52. Ibid. 175.
53. This assertion echoes what George says in the play: " 'And the west, encumbered by crippling alliances, and burdened with morality too rigid to accommodate itself to the swing of events, must ... eventually ... fall' " (174).
54. For more about this specific issue of public and private discourse, see Jody Pennington, "Public Discourse on Marriage & Privacy—Concealment or Revelation?: The Reception of *Who's Afraid of Virginia Woolf?*" *American Studies in Scandinavia* 37.2 (2005): 25–43.
55. More generally, C. W. E. Bigsby suggests (following the fact that the play was onetime called *The Exorcism*) that the play is "concerned with the purgation and ultimate destruction of illusion" ("*Who's Afraid of Virginia Woolf?*: Edward Albee's Morality Play," *Journal of American Studies* 1.2 (1967): 258). Asked about O'Neill's conclusions in *The Iceman Cometh* and Ibsen's stance that "if you take away make-believe from the average man, you take away his happiness as well," Albee "insisted that man's real need was to learn to live with truth" (Bigsby 257).
56. "Terror," *Oxford English Dictionary*, 2nd ed., 1989.
57. "Fear," *Oxford English Dictionary*, 2nd ed., 1989.
58. For a longer discussion on the Theatre of the Absurd in regard to history and an outlook on the future, see Michael Y. Bennett, *Reassessing the Theatre of the Absurd: Camus, Beckett, Ionesco, Genet, and Pinter* (New York: Palgrave Macmillan, 2011) 14–20.
59. Albee, *Virginia Woolf?* 67.
60. Though this is play about a more or less privileged class of white people in New England, there is also the question of race (i.e., extending

from the emergence of the Civil Rights movement) that sneaks its way into the play. Nick represents, at least to George, the threat and appeal (to others) of white supremacy, of a "super-civilization" that is a remnant of the Nazi's dream of an Aryan race and a (generally) racist American South:

> I suspect we will not have much music, much painting, but we will have a civilization of men, smooth, blond, and right at the middleweight limit.
>
> (Albee, *Virginia Woolf?* 66)

Nick, who is blond and still "at the middleweight limit," displays no bigoted views in the play himself. However, he representation through his focus on biology alerts George (and the viewers) to the fact that

> ...diversity will no longer be the goal. Cultures and races will eventually vanish...the ants will take over the world.
>
> (Ibid. 67)

61. Here I disagree with James P. Quinn who suggests that, in parodying a romance, *Virginia Woolf?'s* Nick and Honey show little difference from the older generation (George and Martha) in that both couples are like "automaton conformists" and live a "meaningless, unauthentic existence" ("Myth and Romance in Albee's Who's Afraid of Virginia Woolf" *Arizona Quarterly: A Journal of American Literature, Culture, and Theory* 30 (1974): 200). Martha and George are in no way "conformists."
62. Albee, *Stretching My Mind* 15–16.
63. Albee, Virginia Woolf? 66.
64. Albee, *Stretching My Mind* 7–12.
65. One can also say that Albee pays homage to Pinter in this play, too. Elsewhere I discuss Martha's psychology as an archetypal childless-wife in relation to Meg in Harold Pinter's *The Birthday Party*. The two plays have an eerily similar plot: "an unhappy childless-wife has a bad relationship with her husband mostly due to the fact that they are childless and turns to a fake son to find comfort; the fake son is then symbolically *killed*, if you will, and the husband is there at the end of the play to provide comfort" (Bennett 66).
66. Albee, *Virginia Woolf?* 7.
67. Ibid.
68. Ibid. 16.
69. Ibid.
70. Ibid. 30.
71. Ibid. 3.

72. Ibid.
73. For a lengthy description of the production history of *Who's Afraid of Virginia Woolf?* and how the power balance between George and Martha has been displayed in different productions, see Bottoms 118–186.
74. Charles Isherwood, "Theater Review: 'Who's Afraid of Virginia Woolf?': Watch It, Martha: This George is a Stealth Bomb," *The New York Times*, December 12, 2010.
75. Katherine E. Kelly, "Review of *Who's Afraid of Virginia Woolf?*" *Theatre Journal* 42.3 (October 1990): 372.
76. Ibid. 222.

CONCLUSION

1. Edward Albee, *Who's Afraid of Virginia Woolf?* (New York: Signet, 1983) 222.
2. This interview was conducted on September 22, 2011, by video conferencing. For thorough descriptions of all of Fusco's performances that we discuss in this interview, see Coco Fusco's website: http://www.thing.net/~cocofusco/work.htm, September 20, 2011.
3. For more about this question and Fusco's answers related to this question, see Dennis Kennedy, *The Spectator and the Spectacle: Audiences in Modernity and Postmodernity* (Cambridge: Cambridge University Press, 2009).
4. See the section in the introduction, "The Theatrical Tension between Rationalism and Empiricism," 4–8.
5. Again, see "The Theatrical Tension between Rationalism and Empiricism," in the introduction.
6. See the last paragraph of "The Theatrical Tension between Rationalism and Empiricism," in the introduction, 7–8.

Bibliography

Albee, Edward. *Stretching My Mind.* New York: Carroll & Graf Publishers, 2005.
——. *Who's Afraid of Virginia Woolf?* New York: Signet, 1983.
Armitage, Christopher. "Blue China and Blue Moods: Oscar Fashioning Himself at Oxford." *Oscar Wilde: The Man, His Writings, and His World.* Ed. Robert N. Keane. New York: AMS Press, 2003, 15–24.
Aronson, Ronald. *Camus and Sartre: The Story of a Friendship and the Quarrel That Ended It.* Chicago, IL: The University of Chicago Press, 2004.
Artaud, Antonin. "The Theatre of Cruelty." *The Theory of the Modern Stage: An Introduction to Modern Theatre and Drama.* Ed. Eric Bentley. Middlesex: Penguin Books, 1970.
Barth, Adolf. "Oscar Wilde's 'Comic Refusal': A Reassessment of *The Importance of Being Earnest.*" *Archiv für das Studium der neueren Sprachen und Literaturen* 216 (1979): 120–128.
Baumrin, Seth. "No Longer in Search of an Author, a Character Defines Herself: Pirandello's *Six Characters in Search of an Author* and Eugenio Barba's Experimental Performance Methodology." *Modern Drama* 44.2 (2001): 174–187.
Beckett, Samuel. *En attendant Godot.* Paris: Les Éditions de Minuit, 1952.
——. *Waiting for Godot.* New York: Grove Press, 1954.
Bennett, Michael Y. "Brecht in the Wilde: *Salomé*'s Liminal Spaces and the Storyteller." *Journal of Theatre and Drama* 7/8 (2001): 145–158.
——. " 'The Essential Doesn't Change': Essence Precedes Experience and Cartesian Rationalism in Samuel Beckett's *Waiting for Godot.*" *Notes on Contemporary Literature* 42.1 (January 2012): 5–7.
——. *Reassessing the Theatre of the Absurd: Camus, Beckett, Ionesco, Genet, and Pinter.* New York: Palgrave Macmillan, 2011.
——. Review of *Waiting for Godot. Theatre Journal* 62.1 (March 2010): 110–111.

———. "Sartre's 'The Wall' and Beckett's *Waiting for Godot*: Existential and Non-Existential Nothingness." *Notes on Contemporary Literature* 39.5 (November 2009): 2–3.

Bigsby, C. W. E. "*Who's Afraid of Virginia Woolf?*: Edward Albee's Morality Play." *Journal of American Studies* 1.2 (1967): 257–268.

Borstelmann, Thomas. *The Cold War and the Color Line: American Race Relations in the Global Arena.* Cambridge: Harvard University Press, 2001.

Boschetti, Anna. *The Intellectual Enterprise: Sartre and Les Temps Modernes.* Trans. Richard C. McCleary. Evanston, IL: Northwestern University Press, 1988.

Bosworth, R. J. B. *Mussolini's Italy: Life under the Dictatorship, 1915–1945.* New York: The Penguin Press, 2006.

Bottoms, Stephen J. *Albee: Who's Afraid of Virginia Woolf?* Cambridge: Cambridge University Press, 2000.

Brantley, Ben. " 'Who's Afraid of Virginia Woolf?': Marriage as Blood Sport: A No-Win Game." *The New York Times* March 21, 2005.

Brecht, Bertolt. "A Short Organum for the Theatre." *Brecht on Theatre.* Ed. and Trans. John Willett. New York: Hill and Wang, 1964, 179–208.

Brée, Germaine. *Camus and Sartre: Crisis and Commitment.* New York: Delacorte Press, 1972.

Bryden, Mary. "Deleuze Reading Beckett," *Beckett and Philosophy.* Ed. Richard Lane. New York: Palgrave, 2002.

Camus, Albert. "A Letter to the Editor of *Les Temps modernes*." *Sartre and Camus: A Historic Confrontation.* Ed. and Trans. David A. Sprintzen and Adrian van der Hoven. Amherst, MA: Humanity Books, 2004.

———. *The Rebel: An Essay on Man in Revolt.* New York: Vintage Books, 1956.

Candlish, Stewart. *The Russell/Bradley Dispute and Its Significance for Twentieth-Century Philosophy.* New York: Palgrave Macmillan, 2009.

Carlson, Marvin. *Performance: A Critical Introduction.* 2nd ed. New York: Routledge, 2004.

Carr, Edward Hallett. *The Twenty Years' Crisis: An Introduction to the Study of International Relations.* New York: Harper & Row, Publishers, 1964.

Cassidy, David. *Einstein and Our World.* New Jersey: Humanities Press, 1995.

Catalano, Joseph S. "Successfully Lying to Oneself: A Sartrean Perspective." *Philosophy and Phenomenology Research* 50.4 (January 1990): 673–693.

Catanzaro, Michael R. "From the Country to the City, Buburyists Rise above Societal Conceptions of Good and Evil in the Earnest Pursuit of

Passion." *The Image of the City in Literature, Media, and Society: Selected Papers from the 2003 Conference of the Society for the Interdisciplinary Study of Social Imagery.* Ed. Will Wright and Steven Kaplan. Pueblo, CO: The Society, 2003, 212–217.

Chambers, Timothy. "The Elevator Effect." *Radical Philosophy* 156 (July/August 2009): 56–59.

Chapin, Peter. "Wilde at Oxford/Oxford Gone Wilde," *Reading Wilde: Querying Spaces.* New York: New York University Fales Library, 1995, 27–34.

"Character." *Oxford English Dictionary.* 2nd ed., 1989.

Cohen-Solal, Annie. *Sartre: A Life.* Trans. Anna Cancogni. Ed. Norman Macafee. New York: Pantheon Books, 1987.

Copelston, Frederick. *Contemporary Philosophy: Studies of Logical Positivism and Existentialism.* London: Continuum, 1972.

———. *A History of Philosophy: Volume VIII: Modern Philosophy: Empiricism, Idealism, and Pragmatism in Britain and America.* New York: Image Books, 1966.

Cotter, Holland. "A Broken City. A Tree. Evening." *The New York Times* December 2, 2007.

Cousineau, Thomas. "Descartes, Lacan, and *Murphy.*" *College Literature* 11.3 (1984): 223–232.

———. "Watt: Language as Interdiction and Consolation." *The Beckett Studies Reader.* Ed. S. E. Gontarski. Gainsville, FL: University Press of Florida, 1993.

Davies, Telory W. "Performance Review of *Rhinoceros.*" *Theatre Journal* 54.4 (December 2002): 645–646.

Davis, Tracy C. and Thomas Postlewait, "Theatricality: An Introduction." *Theatricality.* Ed. Tracy C. Davis and Thomas Postlewait. Cambridge: Cambridge University Press, 2004.

Deans, Jill R. "Albee's Substitute Children: Reading Adoption as a Performance." *Journal of Dramatic Theory and Criticism* 13.2 (Spring 1999): 57–79.

de Saussure, Ferdinand. *Course in General Linguistics.* Ed. Charles Bally and Albert Sechehaye. Trans. Roy Harris. Chicago, IL: Open Court, 2000.

"Disposition." *Oxford English Dictionary.* 2nd ed., 1989.

Donohue, Joseph. "*Salome* and the Wildean Art of Symbolist Theatre." *Modern Drama* 37.1 (1994): 84–103.

Drake, David. *Intellectuals and Politics in Post-War France.* London: Palgrave, 2002.

Ducker, Dan. " 'Pow!' 'Snap!' 'Pouf!': The Modes of Communication in *Who's Afraid of Virginia Woolf?*" *CLA Journal* 26.4 (June 1983): 465–477.

Dudziak, Mary L.. *Cold War Civil Rights: Race and the Image of American Democracy*. Princeton, NJ: Princeton University Press, 2000.

Eby, Claire Virginia. "Fun and Games with George and Nick: Competitive Masculinity in *Who's Afraid of Virginia Woof?*" *Modern Drama* 50.4 (Winter 2007): 601–618.

Eksteins, Modris. *Rites of Spring: The Great War and the Birth of the Modern Age*. New York: Anchor Books, 1989.

Ellmann, Richard. *Oscar Wilde*. New York: Alfred A. Knopf, 1988.

———. *Oscar Wilde at Oxford*. Washington, D.C.: Library of Congress, 1984.

Esslin, Martin. *The Theatre of the Absurd*. Garden City, NY: Anchor Books, 1961.

Farber, Vreneli. "Review of *Waiting for Godot*." *Theatre Journal* 53.4 (December 2001): 653–655.

"Fear." *Oxford English Dictionary*. 2nd ed., 1989.

Fforde, Matthew. *Conservatism and Collectivism, 1886–1914*. Edinburgh: Edinburgh University Press, 1990.

Fisher, Dominique D. *Staging of Language and Language(s) of the Stage: Marllarmé's Poëme Critique and Artaud's Poetry-Minus-Text*. New York: Peter Lang, 1994.

Flasch, Joy. "Games People Play in *Who's Afraid of Virginia Woolf?*" *Modern Drama* 10 (1967): 280–288.

Forsdick, Charles. "Camus and Sartre: The Great Quarrel." *The Cambridge Companion to Camus*. Ed. Edward J. Hughes. Cambridge: Cambridge University Press, 2007, 118–130.

Freeman, Sara. "Review of *The Importance of Being Earnest* and *Travesties*." *Theatre Journal* 58.2 (May 2006): 656–658.

French, Michael. *US Economic History Since 1945*. Manchester: Manchester University Press, 1997.

Fusco, Coco. Video Conference Interview. September 22, 2011.

Gaddis, John Lewis. *The Cold War: A New History*. New York: Penguin Books, 2005.

"Georg Wilhelm Friedrich Hegel," *Stanford Encyclopedia of Philosophy*, http://plato.stanford.edu/entries/hegel, February 6, 2011.

Gibson, Andrew. "Beckett and Badiou." *Beckett and Philosophy*. Ed. Richard Lane. New York: Palgrave, 2002.

Giudice, Gaspare. *Pirandello: A Biography*. Trans. Alastair Hamilton. London: Oxford University Press, 1975.

Gregg, Pauline. *A Social and Economic History of Britain: 1760–1965*. London: George G. Harrap & Co. Ltd., 1965.

Gregor, A. James. *Mussolini's Intellectuals: Fascist Social and Political Thought*. Princeton, NJ: Princeton University Press, 2005.

Hampton, Wilborn. "Review/Theater 'The Importance of Being Earnest.'" *The New York Times* March 18, 1990.

Howells, Christina, ed. *The Cambridge Companion to Sartre*. Cambridge: Cambridge University Press, 1992.

Hughes, Edward J. *The Cambridge Companion to Camus*. Cambridge: Cambridge University Press, 2007.

Huizinga, Johan. *Homo Ludens: A Study of the Play-Element in Culture*. London: Beacon, 1955.

Hutcheon, Linda and Michael Hutcheon. " 'Here's Looking at You Kid': The Empowering Gaze in *Salome*." *Profession* (1998): 11–22.

Isherwood, Charles. "Lady Bracknell is Back, With a Slightly Unladylike Air." *The New York Times* August 26, 2009.

———. " 'Who's Afraid of Virginia Woolf?': Watch It, Martha: This George is a Stealth Bomb." *The New York Times* December 12, 2010.

James, Caryn. "A Thoroughly Modern Oscar and Algernon." *The New York Times* May 7, 2008.

James, Henry. *The Golden Bowl*. Ed. Virginia Llewellyn Smith. Oxford: Oxford University Press, 2009.

Jeanson, Francis. "Albert Camus, of the Soul in Revolt." *Sartre and Camus: A Historic Confrontation*. Ed. and Trans. David A. Sprintzen and Adrian van der Hoven. Amherst, MA: Humanity Books, 2004.

Jones, Howard. *The Bay of Pigs*. Oxford: Oxford University Press, 2008.

Judt, Tony. *Past Imperfect: French Intellectuals, 1944–1954*. Berkeley, CA: University of California Press, 1992.

———. *Postwar: A History of Europe Since 1945*. New York: Penguin Books, 2005.

Kelly, Katherine E. "Review of *Who's Afraid of Virginia Woolf?*" *Theatre Journal* 42.3 (October 1990): 372–373.

Kelly, Michael. *The Cultural and Intellectual Rebuilding of France after the Second World War*. Houndsmills: Palgrave Macmillan, 2004.

Kennedy, Dennis. *The Spectator and the Spectacle: Audiences in Modernity and Postmodernity*. Cambridge: Cambridge University Press, 2009.

Klein, Alvin. "Theater: A Play for a Past Century, This One and the Next." *The New York Times* October 31, 1999.

Lalonde, Jeremy. "A 'Revolutionary Outrage': *The Importance of Being Earnest* as Social Criticism." *Modern Drama* 48.4 (Winter 2005): 659–676.

Lester, Michèle. "Through the Looking Glass: Beckett." *Anamnesia: Private and Public Memory in Modern French Culture*. Ed. Peter Collier and Anna Magdalena Elsner. Bern: Peter Lang, 2009.

Lottmann, Herbert R. *The Left Bank: Writers, Artists, and Politics from the Popular Front to the Cold War.* Boston, MA: Houghton Mifflin Company, 1982.

Luere, Jeane. "Terror and Violence in Edward Albee?: From *Who's Afraid of Virginia Woolf?* To Marriage Play." *South Central Review* 7.1 (Spring 1990): 50–58.

Maude, Ulrika. "The Body of Memory: Beckett and Merleau-Ponty." *Beckett and Philosophy.* Ed. Richard Lane. New York: Palgrave, 2002.

McAuley, Gay. *Space in Performance: Making Meaning in the Theatre.* Ann Arbor, MI: The University of Michigan Press, 2000.

Meche, Jude. "Beckett's *Not I*: Empty Speech and Obsession in Mouth's Dialogue." *Studies in the Humanities* 25.1-2 (1998): 101–111.

Milward, Alan S. *The Reconstruction of Western Europe: 1945–1951.* Berkeley, CA: University of California Press, 1984.

Moorjani, Angela. "Beckett and Psychoanalysis." *Palgrave Advances in Samuel Beckett Studies.* Ed. Lois Oppenheim. New York: Palgrave Macmillan, 2004.

Northrop, F. S. C. "Leibniz's Theory of Space." *Journal of the History of Ideas* 7.4 (October 1946): 422–446.

Oliver, Roger W. *Dreams of Passion: The Theater of Luigi Pirandello.* New York: New York University Press, 1979.

"Ooze." *Oxford English Dictionary.* 2nd ed., 1989.

Overy, R. J. *The Inter-War Crisis 1919–1939.* 2nd ed. Harlow, England: Pearson Longman, 2007.

Paolucci, Anne "Comedy and Paradox in Pirandello's Plays (An Hegelian Perspective)." *The Plays and Fiction of Luigi Pirandello: Selected Essays.* Ed. Anne Paolucci. New York: Griffon House Publications, 2009.

———. *Pirandello's Theater: The Recovery of the Modern Stage for Dramatic Art.* Carbondale: Southern Illinois University Press, 1974.

Patterson, James T. *Grand Expectations: The United States, 1945–1974.* New York: Oxford University Press, 1996.

Paul, Louis. "A Game Analysis of Albee's *Who's Afraid of Virginia Woolf?*: The Core of Grief." *Literature and Psychology* 17 (1967): 47–51.

Pennington, Jody. "Public Discourse on Marriage & Privacy—Concealment or Revelation?: The Reception of Who's Afraid of Virginia Woolf?" *American Studies in Scandinavia* 37.2 (2005): 25–43.

Petruzzi, Anthony. "Hermeneutic Retrieval and the Conflict of Styles in Pirandello's *Sei Personaggi in Cerca D'Autore*." *RSQ: Rhetoric Society Quarterly* 27.3 (Summer 1997): 51–83.

Pirandello, Luigi. *Six Characters in Search of an Author.* Trans. Edward Storer. Mineola, NY: Dover Publications, Inc., 1998.

Pollmann, Leo. *Sartre and Camus: Literature of Existence*. Trans. Helen and Gregor Sebba. New York: Frederik Ungar Publishing Co., 1970.
Pyle, Forest. "Extravagance; Or, Salomé's Kiss." *The Journal of Pre-Raphaelite Studies* 7 (1998): 39–52.
Quinn, James P. "Myth and Romance in Albee's *Who's Afraid of Virginia Woolf?*" *Arizona Quarterly: A Journal of American Literature, Culture, and Theory* 30 (1974): 197–204.
Rich, Frank. "Review: Theater Soviet Director Puts the Audience into 'Six Characters.' " *The New York Times* July 24, 1989.
Robertson, C. Warren. "An Analysis of *Who's Afraid of Virginia Woolf?*" *Publications of the Mississippi Philological Association* (1986): 112–120.
Ross, Kristin. *Fast Cars, Clean Bodies: Decolonization and the Reordering of French Culture*. Cambridge: The MIT Press, 1996.
Roudané, Matthew. "*Who's Afraid of Virginia Woolf?*: Toward the Marrow." *The Cambridge Companion to Edward Albee*. Ed. Stephen Bottoms. Cambridge: Cambridge University Press, 2005.
Royle, Peter. *The Sartre-Camus Controversy: A Literary and Philosophical Critique*. Ottawa: University of Ottawa Press, 1982.
Sartre, Jean-Paul. *Being and Nothingness: A Phenomenological Essay on Ontology*. Trans. Hazel E. Barnes. New York: Washington Square, 1984.
———. "Existentialism is a Humanism." *Existentialism: From Dostoevsky to Sartre*. Ed. Walter Kaufman. New York: Plume Book, 1975.
———. "Reply to Albert Camus." *Sartre and Camus: A Historic Confrontation*. Ed. and Trans. David A. Sprintzen and Adrian van den Hoven. Amherst, MA: Humanity Books, 2004.
Siegel, Naomi. "Redgrave Leads an 'Earnest' That Delights the Eye and Ear." *The New York Times* January 24, 2009.
Shakespeare, William. *Hamlet*. Ed. Barbara A Mowat and Paul Werstine. New York: Washington Square, 1992.
Smith, A. D. "Space and Sight." *Mind* 109.435 (July 2000): 481–518.
Smith II, Philip E. and Michael S. Helfand, eds. *Oscar Wilde's Oxford Notebooks: A Portrait of Mind in the Making*. New York: Oxford University Press, 1989.
Snider, Clifton. "Synchronicity and the Trickster in *The Importance of Being Earnest*." *The Wildean* 27 (2005): 55–63.
Soames, Scott. *Philosophical Analysis in the Twentieth Century: Volume 1: The Dawn of Analysis*. Princeton, NJ: Princeton University Press, 2003.
———. *Philosophical Analysis in the Twentieth Century: Volume 2: The Age of Meaning*. Princeton, NJ: Princeton University Press, 2003.

States, Bert O. "The Actor's Presence: Three Phenomenal Modes." *Acting (Re)Considered: A Theoretical and Practical Guide.* Ed. Philip B. Zarrilli. 2nd ed. London: Routledge, 2002.

———. *Great Reckonings in Little Rooms: On the Phenomenology of the Theater.* Berkeley: University of California Press, 1985.

"Stay." *Oxford English Dictionary.* 2nd ed., 1989.

Stroll, Avrum. *Twentieth-Century Analytic Philosophy.* New York: Columbia University Press, 2000.

Taylor, A. J. P. *The Struggle for Mastery in Europe: 1848–1918.* London: Oxford University Press, 1974.

"Temperament." *Oxford English Dictionary.* 2nd ed., 1989.

"Terror." *Oxford English Dictionary.* 2nd ed., 1989.

Thayer, H. S. *Meaning and Action: A Critical History of Pragmatism.* Indianapolis, IN: The Bobbs-Merrill Company, Inc., 1968.

Van Gelder, Lawrence. "Theater Review: Wilde's Vitorian Wit Dumbed Down in Drag." *The New York Times* July 5, 2003.

Vanhoutte, Jacqueline. "*Salome's* Earnestness." *Text and Presentation* 13 (1992): 83–87.

Wilde, Oscar. *The Importance of Being Earnest and Other Plays.* Ed. Peter Raby. Oxford: Oxford University Press, 2008.

———. *Notebook on Philosophy: 1874–1878,* held at the William Andrews Clark Memorial Library, UCLA [Wilde W6721M3 N9113 [1876/8] Bound.

———. "The Truth of Masks." *Intentions.* Amherst, NY: Prometheus Books, 2004.

Wittgenstein, Ludwig. *Philosophical Investigations: The English Text of the Third Edition.* Trans. G. E. M. Anscombe. New York: Macmillan Publishing Co., Inc., 1958.

Wright, Thomas. *Oscar's Books.* London: Chatto & Windus, 2008.

Yanal, Robert J. "Self-Deception and the Experience of Fiction." *Ratio* 20 (2007): 108–121.

Index

Appia, Adolphe, 12–13
Aron, Raymond, 89
Artaud, Antonin, 12–14
Austin, J. L., 105, 109, 110, 111, 125
Ayer, A. J., 109

"Baby Boomers", 107
"Bad Faith", 27–56
Barth, Adolf, 47–8
Bauman, Richard, 17, 39–40, 133–4
Baumrin, Seth, 68
"Bay of Pigs", 106–7
Bedford, Brian, 38–9
Blau, Herbert, 8, 9
Bottoms, Stephen, J., 105
Bradley, F. H., 32, 34, 54–5, 108
Butusov, Yuri, 91

Camus, Albert, 8, 9, 84–9
Carr, Edward Hallett, 58
Cartwright, David, E., 66
Cassidy, David, 60–1
Castro, Fidel, 106
Catalano, Joseph, S., 49
Chambers, Timothy, 49
Chan, Paul, 92
Chaudhuri, Una, 10
Civil Rights (USA), 108
colonialism, 29, 83

Copleston, 21–32
Croce, Benedetto, 64, 67–8, 78

Dadaism, 61
David, Larry, 112
Davis, Tracy, C., 21–3
Deans, Jill, R., 104
Descartes, Rene, 87
Drake, David, 84

Einstein, Albert, 60
Eksteins, Modris, 61
Esslin, Martin, 90

Fforde, Matthew, 29–30, 37, 46, 55
Fisher, Dominique, Q., 13
Fontana, Santino, 38–9
Foucault, Michel, 7, 55
"Fourth Wall", 4, 57, 113
Freeman, Sara, 38
Frege, Gottlob, 109
Furr, David, 38–9
Fusco, Coco, 126–33

Gaddis, John Lewis, 107
Garner, Jr. Stanton, B., 9–10
"Gaze", 27–56
Gentile, Giovanni, 64, 65–6
Giudice, Gaspare, 66, 68, 70
Goffman, Erving, 133
Gómez-Peña, Guillermo, 126, 128, 130, 132

The Good Person of Szechwan, 45, 48, 134
Green, T. H., 31–2

Hamlet, 1, 2, 5–7, 11, 27, 133–4
Heidegger, Martin, 16, 78–80
Huizinga, Johan, 42, 125
Hume, David, 31–2, 35
Hutcheon, Linda and Michael Hutcheon, 51
Huxley, T. H., 35

idealism
  British (Hegelian), 31–3, 36, 66, 71, 108
  Italian, 63, 64–6, 68, 69, 73, 78
The Importance of Being Earnest, 27–8, 35–50, 54–6, 134
Isherwood, Charles, 121
Italian Fascism, 59, 62, 63, 66, 68

Jeanson, Francis, 87–9
Jowett, Benjamin, 31, 34
Judt, tony, 81–4

Kelly, Katherine, E., 121
Kennedy, John, F., 105–7, 108
Khrushchev, Nikita, 106–7
Klein, Alvin, 37

Lacan, Jacques, 4, 100
Lalonde, Jeremy, 45
logical positivism, 109–10
Luere, Jean, 103

Mahaffy, J. P., 33
"Marshall Plan", 82
materialism, 33
McAuley, Gay, 1, 10

Merleau-Ponty, Maurice, 81, 84
mimesis, 14, 21–3
Müller, F. Max, 33
Mussolini, Benito, 59, 62, 63, 66, 68

Oliver, Roger, W., 69, 71
Overy, R. J., 58–9, 61

Page, Anthony, 91–2
Panunzio, Sergio, 64–5, 78
Paolucci, Anne, 70
Papini, Giovanni, 63–4
Pater, Walter, 33–4
performance
  Actor-Audience Relationship, 18, 54, 133–4
  Insincere Performance, 27–56, 134
  Performer-Audience Relationship, 17–18, 133–4
"performative", 105, 111–23
Petruzzi, Anthony, 78–80
Phelan, Peggy, 131
Postlewait, Thomas, 21–3
pragmatism, 63, 66, 69, 73, 78
Prezzolini, Giuseppe, 63–4
Pyle, Forest, 51

Quine, W. V., 109

Roundabout Theatre Company, 38–9
Royle, Peter, 86
Ruskin, John, 33–4
Russell, Bertrand, 108–9
Russian Revolution, 59

Salome, 27–8, 50–6
Sartre, Jean-Paul, 8, 9, 40–2, 84–9

Saussure, Ferdinand de, 14
Sellars, Wilfrid, 109
Six Characters in Search of an Author, 57–80
Smith, A. D., 19
Smokey Joe's Café, 3–4, 11–12
Snider, Clifton, 44–5
socialism, 29, 37
Spengler, Oswald, 59
States, Bert, O., 2, 10, 15, 21, 134

Les Temps modernes, 81, 84, 87–9
Thayer, H. S., 63
theatricality, 21–3
"Truth of Masks", 34–5

Vanhoutte, Jacqueline, 44
Vienna Circle, 108, 109

Wagner, Richard, 12
Waiting for Godot, 9, 11, 81–101, 104, 117, 119
Whitehead, Alfred North, 109
Who's Afraid of Virginia Woolf?, 103–24
Wittgenstein, Ludwig, 104–5, 108, 109, 110–11

Yanal, Robert, J., 40–1

The Zoo Story, 116

GPSR Compliance

The European Union's (EU) General Product Safety Regulation (GPSR) is a set of rules that requires consumer products to be safe and our obligations to ensure this.

If you have any concerns about our products, you can contact us on

ProductSafety@springernature.com

In case Publisher is established outside the EU, the EU authorized representative is:

Springer Nature Customer Service Center GmbH
Europaplatz 3
69115 Heidelberg, Germany

www.ingramcontent.com/pod-product-compliance
Lightning Source LLC
LaVergne TN
LVHW051911060526
838200LV00004B/93